The
Child
Friendly
Church

The

Church

---

150 Models
of Ministry
with
Children

Boyce A. Bowdon

ABINGDON PRESS
Nashville

THE CHILD-FRIENDLY CHURCH

Library of Congress Cataloging-in-Publication Data

Bowdon, Boyce A., 1935–
    The child friendly church: 150 models of ministry with children / Boyce A. Bowdon.
      p.   cm.
    ISBN 0-687-07574-2 (alk. paper)
      1. Church work with children—United Methodist Church (U.S.)—Case studies. 2. Church work with the poor—United Methodist Church (U.S.)—Case studies.   I. Title
    BX8347.B68   1999   99-17228
    259'.22—dc21   CIP

00 01 02 03 04 05 06 07 08 —10 9 8 7 6 5 4 3 2

MANUFACTURED IN THE UNITED STATES OF AMERICA

To my wife
Arlene,

and to our children
Melody and Gina

Acknowledgments

This resource began as a book for my bishop, Bruce Blake, to use in seminars with clergy of the Oklahoma Area concerning the United Methodist Episcopal Initiative on Children and Poverty. Bishop Blake has encouraged me to expand the book and make it available to a larger audience. I am grateful to him for helping me develop this resource.

Bishop Marshall Meadors Jr., chair of the Bishops' Initiative on Children and Poverty, has encouraged and supported me from the beginning of my research.

Also, I am grateful to my communications colleagues across the nation who have brought to my attention outstanding ministries in their areas. Special thanks go to Shirley Struchen and Tom McAnally of United Methodist Communications, and to the following conference editors: Paul Widicus, Illinois Great River Area; Tom Slack, West Ohio Conference; Charlene Bailey, Kansas West Conference; Kathy Noble, Kansas West Conference; Doug Cannon, Southwest Texas Conference; Alvin Horton, Virginia Conference; Mark Westmoreland, North and South Georgia Conferences; Cathy Farmer, Memphis Conference; Jane Dennis, Arkansas Area; and Michael Stanton-Rich, Mississippi Conference director of communication.

Peggy Halsey and Linda Bales and several other leaders of United Methodist general boards have given me leads, and so have conference directors of children's ministries and coordinators of the Episcopal Initiative.

Most of all, I am grateful to the scores of clergy and lay people in child-friendly churches across the country who have allowed me to share with you their inspiring models for children's ministry.

Contents

Part Four: Ministry to Children in Economic Poverty 105

Part Five: Characteristics of a Child-Friendly Church 133

Introduction

Daily news reports remind us that growing up in today's world is tough for children. They need all the help they can get, especially from churches that have so much to offer.

That's why, in 1995, the United Methodist Council of Bishops issued their Episcopal Initiative on Children and Poverty. They wanted to rally support for kids, so they urged the church to reflect on our basic theological grounding, our Wesleyan heritage, our mission, and to respond decisively to the crisis among children and the impoverished.

The Initiative contains this statement: *As the body of Christ, the church is to be a sign, foretaste, and instrument of God's reign in the world. The church, therefore, must identify with those with whom Christ identifies and to whom he ministers. Indeed, the faithfulness of the church is measured by the presence of and response to "the least of these," especially to children and to the poor.*

What can churches do to respond decisively to the crisis among children and the impoverished and really make a difference in their lives?

You'll find answers to that question in this book. It shows and tells how United Methodist churches of various sizes and settings are faithfully ministering to and with children and the impoverished. In fact, you'll find 150 models (specific examples) of ministries that are transforming the lives of people and churches.

We begin by examing models that help churches attract children and their families. Then we look at models for helping children grow as disciples of Christ, models that enable churches to minister to their communities, and models for ministry to and with the poor. We conclude by reflecting on the models to determine what it takes to make a child-friendly church.

As you examine the models, you will find insights, ideas, and inspiration that will help you and your congregation respond faithfully to our bishops' call—and to God's call.

Part One

Attracting Children to the Church

1.

Dove of the Desert United Methodist Church
GLENDALE, ARIZONA

The pastor and congregation at Dove of the Desert take pride in being a child-friendly church.

"We are always looking for ways to help children know we love them and welcome them into the life of our church," says Mike Pearson, senior pastor of the church, which he founded in 1989 in the suburb of Phoenix.

Many Dove of the Desert members are young couples with children. "I know a lot of our people come here because their kids like our church," says Mike. What attracts them? He points to several models of ministry that have proven effective:

Model 1:
Children have responsibilities in the service.

Children-along with their parents-serve as greeters. Kids greet kids and give them bulletins prepared especially for them, written at their level and featuring information about activities for them. They serve us acolytes and frequently usher.

Model 2:
Children are welcomed at worship services.

"We give the smaller kids activity bags that contain pictures they can color, pencils, crayons, and other items that they can use to entertain themselves," says Mike.

For parents who prefer not to take their children into the sanctuary because they are afraid they might disturb other worshipers, there's a cry room.

Model 3:
The children's sermon is a highlight of the service.

Targeted for children, the children's sermon is also popular with adults. The message always focuses on God's love, how we receive it, and how we share it. And it's presented creatively.

Last summer, Mike invited kids to bring pets as part of the children's sermon. One pet was brought each Sunday, and the children's sermon focused on that one pet, Mike explains. "We had cats, dogs, birds, a pig, a Japanese rooster, one boy even brought his pet snake. Some kids not only brought their pets, they also brought their friends."

How did Mike use the animals to make a point? Here's an example: One Sunday he asked a child what he would do if his dog strayed and got lost. The child quickly replied, "I love him and I'd try to find him!" Mike replied, "God love's us, and when we stray away, God tries to find us too." He followed up with the story Jesus told about the woman who lost a coin and searched for it.

One person who brought a dog to the service said to Mike a few days later, "Fellabear hasn't been the same since I brought him to church. He's so much more relaxed," she quipped.

A puppet ministry is included occasionally as part of the children's sermon to the delight of children and many adults. Mike emphasizes, however, that entertaining the congregation is not an end in itself; it's only a means of presenting God's message.

Model 4:
Third-graders receive Bibles and use them.

When the Scripture is read, the liturgist announces that he or she is reading from the Bible children are given, and invites them to turn to the page in their Bibles and read along silently. Mike says usually more children than adults bring Bibles to worship.

Model 5:
Music ministry keeps children in mind.

"In every worship service we have at least one hymn that children love," Mike says. Their favorites include *This Little Light of Mine, Jesus Loves Me,* and *He's Got the Whole World in His Hands.*

Children's choirs are emphasized. "We have three children's choirs and a youth choir. As a rule they participate once a month in worship," says Mike.

Children participate along with adults in the church's steel drum band, which performs in churches and other settings in the Phoenix area and beyond. "Our youngest band members are nine and our oldest are retirees,"

Mike observes. "This provides enriching intergenerational experiences for all of our people."

Model 6:

Nursery and classrooms are appealing.

Children's rooms are furnished and decorated to appeal to children and their parents. They are clean, sanitary, and safe. Parents who leave infants in the nursery are given pagers, so they can be contacted quickly if their child gets cranky.

Model 7:

Workers with children are good role models.

Sunday school teachers and others who work with children are carefully chosen and well trained. They love children and believe what they do helps children grow.

Model 8:

Children have opportunities to help others.

Kids Helping Kids is a group that encourages children of the church to help other children. For example, they go to a school for homeless children and help them prepare for school, and hang out with them.

Model 9:

Dove of the Desert reaches out to parents.

Mike points out that to attract children, a church obviously has to also attract their parents.

Like most pastors, he encourages members to invite their friends, relatives, associates, and neighbors. He writes thank-you notes to each member who invites someone to worship and helps members find ways to extend invitations.

Model 10:

Invitations are given to baptisms.

"Anytime we have a baptism—adult or infant—we give the family ten nicely printed invitations to send friends or relatives," Mike explains. "The invitation simply says, `You are invited to share in our joy as (the person's name) receives the sacrament of baptism on (the date of the baptism) at Dove of the Desert United Methodist Church.'"

Model 11:
Yard signs announce births.

We have a yard sign we use anytime a baby is born to members of our congregation," says Mike. "Playing on the name of our church, the sign says: 'Another dove sent from heaven.' Parents of the newborn babies are particularly pleased to have the sign in front of their house. Besides announcing the birth of their child, it gives them a way to tell others that their church means a lot to them and that Dove of the Desert is child friendly."

Model 12:
Dove of the Desert advertises consistently.

"From the very beginning in 1989, we decided that we would put about 5 percent of our annual revenues into advertising," Mike said. "And we continue to invest our financial resources and also our talent and creativity on advertising."

Model 13:
Dove of the Desert sponsors community events.

"We host numerous seminars on a variety of subjects, such as parenting newborns and infants," says Mike. "These events remind people that we are a child-friendly church."

Model 14:
Members do community service.

Dove of the Desert members help the local Ronald McDonald House raise funds for local charities, and collect clothing for the homeless. They've helped build a playground for another church. They sponsor scouting groups and their building is available for Twelve-Step and other groups in the community.

"We do community services because we want to do them and because we ought to do them and because they enable us to serve more people in more ways," Mike explains. "We don't do them just to project an appealing image, but doing them does communicate that we care, that we are part of the community, and that we are child-friendly."

Mike says most children who come to Dove of the Desert soon feel right at home.

"A few Sundays ago, after our worship service, I saw a couple with a child about three years old walking across the parking lot to their car. The little boy was crying. His dad was carrying him. I asked them if the child had gotten hurt. His mother smiled and said, 'No, he's fine. He just doesn't want to leave church.' To me, that's a great testimony. It reassures me that our congregation is child-friendly."

2.

Putnam City United Methodist Church
OKLAHOMA CITY, OKLAHOMA

On the Reverend Robert Gorrell's first Sunday as pastor of Putnam City, only six children were present and four of them belonged to staff members.

Now, five years later, when he invites kids to come forward for the children's sermon, seventy-five or more gather around him. Obviously, he's found some effective ways to attract and involve children in church. Here are some models he values most.

Model 15:
Church is proud of children and shows it.

You walk down the halls and you see enlarged and framed photos of kids having fun. And you also see, taped neatly to walls, pictures drawn and colored in *Kids Club*. The walls remind you of a proud mother's refrigerator door-showcasing her child's masterpieces.

Like Dove of the Desert, featured in chapter 1, Putnam City includes children in the total life of the church. Robert makes this observation: "When we are planning our worship service and when I am preparing my sermon, we not only think of the 55-year-old person who writes the church a nice check every week. We think about the two year old whose father just left her mom, and the six year old whose dad lost his job."

Model 16:
Adults welcome children.

"Children love it when we play an Israeli folk song featuring guitars and other instruments," Robert said. "Some little kids dance in the aisles. The first time they danced, I was afraid some adults would walk out. But I looked around the sanctuary and only saw smiles. After the service several adults said to me: 'We don't understand the music and we don't know why we have to have those other instruments instead of the church organ, but the children are obviously happy, and that makes us happy.'"

Model 17:
Children memorize and recite Scripture.

A special moment in worship services comes when children recite Scripture they have memorized. "Last Sunday, one of our kids stood up during our worship service in front of 350 people, and recited twenty Bible verses without making a single mistake. He just turned four."

Kids are also involved in the church's Wednesday night academy called WOW-Welcome On Wednesdays. The choir director, who has a graduate degree in performing arts, works closely with the kids, helping them do various kinds of theater that they present at WOW and in other settings.

Model 18:
Kids earn points for performance.

"*Church Bucks* is a program some people would not like," Robert acknowledged. "Our kids love it though, and so do I because it rewards significant accomplishments and reinforces good habits. Kids earn points for perfect attendance, bringing a visitor, bringing their Bible, memorizing Scripture, reading a book from the church library and telling their Sunday school class about it, helping their teacher, serving as acolytes, and for other things.

"Their points convert to 'church bucks' that we have printed. We keep a display case filled with toys. At certain times during the year—we try to pick Sundays when we would normally have low attendance—we have Redemption Day. And on those days the kids can exchange their church bucks for toys. Several Sundays during the year, we have double bucks day, when one buck counts as two bucks."

When the stock of toys runs low, calls are made to several church members who support the award program and they promptly contribute more than enough money to replenish the stock.

"Some of our most enthusiastic supporters of church bucks are senior adults," Robert said. "One ninety-year-old woman says, 'Isn't it great that our church is encouraging kids to memorize Bible verses? I can't believe it.'"

Model 19
Adult classes are paired with children's classes.

Sunday school provides excellent opportunities for a church to include and involve children and to build significant relationships between the children and adults, says Robert.

"We assign one adult class to every children's class. The adults buy literature for the children's class and throw parties for them. At Easter, each adult classes conducts an egg hunt for the child's class they support. It's pretty neat to see older adults laughing and having fun as they color eggs, put them in baskets, hide them, and watch kids find them. They also plan birthday parties and Christmas parties and Valentine parties. Since families are often scattered across the country, it's really important for the older adults and the younger children to connect with one another that way. We have a lot of surrogate grandparents and grandchildren."

Model 20:

Girls' Night Out builds supportive relationships.

Robert's wife, Prudy, has developed an activity for women called "Girls' Night Out." The church has about forty women who are under age forty, most of them work. Some are single moms.

Girls' Night Out focuses on developing relationships between the women. "It's a time for fun and fellowship. They elect a president every month," Robert explains, "and the new president's only job is to plan the next party, which usually means deciding which restaurant they will go to for dinner. Girls' Night Out has become a Christian support group that they really count on."

Moms don't have to worry about getting a baby sitter. They bring their children to church and leave them in the care of competent attendants. They have no reason to feel guilty about leaving them or anxious about how they will be treated.

"You'd be surprised how many young families get more involved in our church because of Girls' Night Out," says Robert. "This activity enables us to involve and include more children in our ministry."

Model 21:

Child care is provided for all church happenings.

Any time there's a meeting or any other event at Putnam City, child care is provided.

Robert advises: "To be responsible care givers, we must have clean and safe and attractive facilities for our nursery and Sunday school and day care ministries. And we must staff them with people who love kids and are physically, mentally, emotionally, and spiritually able to care for them."

Putnam City has a director on staff who supervises everybody who works in child care. Kids are not just warehoused. They have things to do that are fun, safe, and enriching.

Model 22:
The church works closely with schools.

"Our lay people have a building on the school grounds where we keep a nice stock of children's shoes," Robert says. "The school counselors give the shoes to children who need them. Every pair has a little tag that says, 'A gift from Putnam City United Methodist Church.' We give away two to three thousand pairs a year. We are also available to the Putnam City counselors as a receiving agency for family needs of any kind."

Model 23:
Lay volunteers help families in need.

Putnam City church's program called "Daily Bread" is operated by lay volunteers.

Robert says: "We help people find a place to stay or clothes or food. But we don't just hand them a sack of rice and beans, and tell them good-bye. Our lay people listen to them and help them connect with helping agencies in the city. It's not at all unusual to see a single mom come in with six kids she trying to support. We help her put food on her table and try to help her find a job. At the very least, we give her emotional and spiritual support."

Several families whose first contact with the church came through the Daily Bread ministry are now members of the church. One who came for emergency assistance is now on the staff.

"The Daily Bread ministry not only is needed by people in our community who are having a tough time," Robert says. "Our church needs it. It does for our lay people who work in it the same thing that going on a mission trip does for our Volunteers-in-Mission teams."

Model 24:
Child Development Center extends the church's ministry.

A key component in Putnam City's ministry to children is its Child Development Center, which has 200 children and a long waiting list.

Robert said: "Our church operates the Child Development Center. It's a major mission for us. We do our best to integrate it with the rest of our church into a single ministry. Parents know this up front, and even those who are unchurched say they like having their children in a church environment."

CDC kids are invited—not pressured—to take part in church activities. For example, at six o'clock every morning for a week before vacation Bible school, a church staff member goes to the CDC and greets parents bringing children for child care, tells them about VBS, and invites them to bring their kids.

Model 25:
The church ministers to CDC families.

"Throughout the year," says Robert, "we invite families of our center to classes on parenting skills, communication skills, step-parenting, chemical dependency, and other subjects.

"We do everything we can to help church parents and CDC parents get acquainted. Those personal relationships are vitally important to integrating the CDC into the life of the church. Our society is largely unchurched, and our CDC families are part of that culture. Many have no other connection with a church. We are certainly in a place to minister to them."

Model 26.
The Child Development Center has a VBS.

Wednesdays during the summer, the CDC uses the United Methodist vacation Bible school curriculum material in all the classes. "Even parents who are not active in any church, are pleased that we are including vacation Bible school material in our curriculum," Robert said.

Model 27:
The Child Development Center has a chaplain.

To help make the CDC a vital part of the church's ministry and to extend the church's ministry to CDC families, Putnam City has a Child Development Center chaplain, Dr. J. C. Curry Jr., a retired United Methodist minister. He tells children Bible stories, leads chapel service, and helps build good relations between the church and the CDC.

Model 28:
Vacation Bible School families receive pastoral care.

"When we get information that a child or some member of a child's family is in the hospital or has some other crisis, our chaplain goes to see about them," Robert said. "He helps them be a little more aware that God loves them and is always with them."

The church also keeps up with the children's birthdays, and faithfully contacts them by phone or with a card. "I'm kind of a granddaddy to lots of them," the chaplain explains. "Many of the kids come from homes that have been divided by divorce or death, and they just have one parent who is active in their lives.

3.

First United Methodist Church
HOBBS, NEW MEXICO

"Young families are particular about where they leave their children and they should be," declares Mary McVay, who was children's director from 1991 until 1998 at First Church.

"Anything you can do to help parents realize that young children are important to your church, helps them feel more comfortable and more welcomed. And one of the best things you can do to attract and involve children is to make their classrooms as appealing as possible."

Mary speaks from experience. She remembers when Hobbs children "got stuck with a dull and dingy basement that felt like a dungeon" as the setting for their nursery through kindergarten Sunday school classes, the weekday playschool, and the mother's day out.

All that changed in 1991, thanks to Kara Wink, the director of the mother's day out. Kara, Mary recalls, was looking at a Noah's ark picture book when she dreamed up an idea: Why not turn the depressing room into a bright and cheerful Noah's ark?

Kara visualized creating a room where kids could stand in the middle and look around at walls with paintings of animals resembling the animals in the picture book.

Her idea appealed to church officials, parents, and children-all of whom were eager to make the children's area more attractive. Soon she recruited local artists to draw outlines of animals. Then crews of youth and adults filled in the outlines.

"All the paint was donated," says Mary. "Once the project got underway, new ideas evolved. We put up fun signs like you might have seen in the ark. We had a picture of Noah and Mrs. Noah. The boy's bathroom was painted as a money cage and the girl's bathroom was painted as an aquarium."

Before the summer was over, the basement had a new look, Mary says. "No longer did you feel like you were going into a dungeon. You felt like you were going into a fun place designed just for kids. It was alive and gave you a lift."

Model 29:
Attractive facilities attract children and parents.

The transformation of the basement brought about a transformation in the ministry of Hobbs First. "The kids loved it and so did their parents," says Mary. "They saw that children's ministry was a priority for us. It boosted the attendance and involvement of young families. And that caused some good things to happen for our church, as well as for the children and their parents."

4.

Haikey Chapel
BIXBY, OKLAHOMA

For the first time in more than a decade, Haikey Chapel had vacation Bible school in June of 1998.

"It was absolutely wonderful," says Sunrise Ross, the mother of three elementary school-age children who is helping the Native American church near Bixby, on the outskirts of Tulsa, Oklahoma, rebuild its ministry with children. She shared with me the models that are attracting and involving children.

Model 30:
Encourage kids to expect something from church.

"We are trying to get our children to expect things from us. We want them to expect us to have vacation Bible school and to expect us to have Sunday school and to expect us to have children's time during the worship service."

Before Sunrise came to Haikey Chapel in 1994, only two children were attending. "I didn't want to come here," she admits. "They had nothing to offer me as a mother of three." Within a few weeks, Haikey Chapel was appointed a new minister, the Reverend Bernadine Dowdy.

"We started throwing ideas at her before she got unpacked" says Sunrise, "and she was really receptive. We told her that Haikey Chapel was an adult church, that kids had no ownership to anything, and that the church was never going to attract children unless children knew they were wanted and that they had a place."

Bernadine listened and she shared the concerns expressed by Sunrise and other advocates of children's ministry. And she did more than listen.

Model 31:
Make a place for kids and they will come.

"Our pastor challenges us to do more than say we want to do this and we want to do that," says Sunrise. "If we want a children's ministry, then she insists that we do more than talk about it and more than pray about it. She insists on us working at it."

And the folks at Haikey have been working at it. Instead of complaining that there were no children, they started providing Sunday school classes and various activities for children. Kids didn't pack the church over night, but within a couple years the word got around.

"People heard that the Lord was doing all kinds of things here, and Haikey Chapel was starting to come alive again," says Sunrise. "Families just came out of the woodwork. Now we have about twenty-five kids who come regularly."

How did the church help kids begin to expect something from the church? One way was to provide better facilities for children and youth. "There wasn't a classroom for kids," Bernadine explains. "They were meeting in fellowship hall on two tables set aside for them, one for the toddlers and one for the other kids who were up to eleven years old. With all the people coming in and out of fellowship hall during Sunday school, they were distracted. They couldn't get into any depth in their study. They needed classrooms, and we knew it."

Led by their pastor, the congregation found information and made contacts that led to securing help from United Methodist Volunteers-in-Mission, who worked alongside members of Haikey Chapel to build a Christian education addition that would provide space for two classrooms, which could be divided into two additional rooms.

"Five or six VIM teams from across America came to help us," Sunrise said. "Within four days the first work team had the structure up, and the other teams finished the job, installing electricity, plumbing, heating, and air. We were in awe."

There was still work to be done on June 6, 1998, when Haikey Chapel's VBS began. But finished or not, the third- and fourth-graders met in one room and the fifth- and sixth-graders met in the other.

"Those kids are so proud of their rooms and so excited about our church," says Sunrise. From the sound of her voice as she told me about plans for starting a children's choir, she was pretty proud and excited herself.

She concludes: "Do something that let's kids see you are serious about ministering to and with them."

Part Two

Helping Children Grow as Disciples

5.

First United Methodist Church
SALEM, OREGON

"Our ministries are not all that unusual, but we are doing a lot of things very intentionally to help children grow as disciples."

That's how the associate pastor, the Reverend Jane Shaffer, describes children's ministry of First Church.

Salem, the capitol of Oregon, is a city of 125,000 in an agricultural valley with a growing number of industries. The church has about 1,000 members-worship attendance averages 450.

Model 32:
Church teaches children how to worship.

In the pew racks, there's a flyer that suggests ways to include children in the worship experience.

Every two years, Jane leads a training class for parents and children in the kindergarten through the second grade. "It's a daylong workshop," Jane says." We look at worship and being part of the worshiping community, and we do some skills development and worship etiquette training."

Model 33:
Children receive booklet explaining the service.

An eight-page booklet entitled *God's Children Worship: A Guide to Worship for Children, Their Families, and Friends,* is distributed. It describes each element in the worship service from the prelude through the postlude. For example, here's what the booklet says about the offering: "We give our gifts to God. God has given us blessings which we enjoy. Our gift of money is one way of saying thank you to God. Our gifts help the church to do God's work."

The booklet gives a description children can understand of Communion and baptism, and tells why we use different colors for the changing seasons of the year."

Model 34:
Bible Zone curriculum stimulates interest and learning.

Salem First uses *Bible Zone* curriculum for preschool through older elementary classes. Produced by The United Methodist Publishing House and available through Cokesbury, it comes with a teacher's book, a box of toys, and other learning resources.

"*Bible Zone* is wonderful," says Jane. "The material is very hands-on and interactive. Children play games, tell stories, sing, and do all kinds of activities that reiterate the Bible story. Teachers love it because it is right there for them with lots of options. Parents tell me their kids are coming home knowing what the story was and talking about it. It's made a big difference in our attendance in Sunday school and is reducing the burn-out factor for teachers.

Model 35:
The children's fellowship group builds relationships.

To help older elementary children build relationships and prepare for United Methodist Youth Fellowship, the church has a fellowship time for fourth- and fifth-graders. Called Funtastixs, the group meets when UMYF does each week. Along with fun and games, they have learning and spiritual-growth experiences and do mission projects.

"Being a downtown church, we pull kids from several different schools so they don't all know one another," Jane says. "This is another opportunity for them to get better acquainted than they do in Sunday school."

Model 36:
The Sunday school class focuses on parents' concerns.

To help parents sharpen their parenting skills and support one another, the church has an ongoing class every Sunday during the church-school time. It began a decade ago, and attendance ranges from fifteen to twenty-five.

Family Matters is the name of the class. "Anything that has to do with families is a potential topic for this group," Jane says. Not only does it explore ways parents can nurture the physical, mental, emotional, and spiritual growth of their children, it also considers how couples can strengthen their marriages, communicate with each other better, manage their finances, cope with the stress of parenting, and relate to aging parents.

Books, videos, and other resources are used by the class. Professionals in family matters occasionally lead discussion. Sometimes a class member who has expertise on a topic will teach a four- or five-week course.

Jane says the class helps build relationships and becomes a strong support group, especially for young parents who discover they have many concerns and interests in common.

Model 37:

Save Our Sanity builds support for parents with younger children.

SOS, stands for *Save Our Sanity,* and that's precisely what this fellowship group for parents with younger children seeks to do, Jane explains. It meets monthly. Child care is always provided. Sometimes only the parents meet. Other times—when there's a picnic in the park—children come too. Members take turns planning the meetings. Topics range from a night at the movies to having a guest speaker talk about a mutual concern.

Model 38:

Family retreats strengthen intergenerational relationships.

Every fall, the church sponsors a family retreat. It's the highlight of the year for many families, Jane says.

"We go to Camp Magruder, our United Methodist conference camp and retreat center. It's between a fresh water lake that's part of the camp and the Pacific Coast. So we have a beach and a lake to enjoy. Usually about eighty-five people go. We arrive at the camp Friday evening and leave for home Sunday afternoon. We do an intergenerational Bible study. We divide everybody up so you have groups with toddlers through older folks mixed in. We have everyone look at a Bible passage and discuss it. We worship together. During free time, people make candles or baskets, go boating, or stay on the beach and take in the sun or build sandcastles. Our teenagers work with the little kids and they form closer relationships."

Model 39:

The girls' retreat focuses on spiritual growth.

Every spring, Jane leads a weekend retreat at Camp Macgruder for girls in grades three through seven. "We study the Bible, do skits, and worship," Jane says. "It delights me to see kids in groups of twos or threes studying Scripture, talking about who God is for them, and sharing their thoughts and feelings."

Model 40:
The vacation Bible school offers options.

Since people today like and need options, every summer Salem First has three different vacation Bible schools. Each is held during a different month, thereby fitting into the summer schedules of more families. And each follows a different format, providing more appealing options for children and for leaders as well. Some kids go to all three events, and love them all, Jane says.

"All three of our schools meet during mornings from nine until noon. The trend in many churches is to do them in the evening, but we tried that and it was less successful for us."

Jane says the June VBS is "fairly traditional." During the July school, called Adventure Week, kids rotate from one classroom to the next. Each classroom is a different village, like Nazareth and Bethlehem. In one classroom they will do games for twenty minutes, in the next there will be storytelling for twenty, then they will go to another room for crafts.

"We've been doing Adventure Week for six years, and it is popular," says Jane. "Our teachers like it because they are just preparing one thing for each day. This makes it easier to recruit leaders. Kids think its much neater than the regular VBS. They like moving from one class to the next."

Salem's VBS in August is a music-theater camp. "Our music program people are involved in it and this gives them an opportunity to start working with the kids," Jane explains.

Model 41:
Children are taught the importance of missions.

During VBS, children take on a mission project. Last year they brought packs of pencils and pens and other school supplies to send to children who live in poverty. The church always has a mission project during Lent that involves children.

"About three years ago, we began our Daily Bread Bag Ministry and we are still doing it," Jane said. "We fill a gallon-size ziplock bag with enough nonperishable food for one person for one day. We also put some Scripture resources in the bag and information about our church. The bags are distributed to the homeless and others who need food."

Model 42:
Child care and Christmas workshop brightens Christmas.

Approximately three weeks before Christmas, Salem First has a child care and Christmas workshop.

"Our intention is to help parents have time to do Christmas shopping without the children in toe," Jane says. "While parents are shopping, children from about age three on up come to church and make Christmas gifts to give parents, grandparents, and others."

Model 43:
Learning day teaches kids about Easter.

During spring break week right before Easter, there's a special learning day for children. "We study about the meaning of Lent and Easter, and we also do some crafts and other fun things," Jane says. "It's like a mini-VBS."

Model 44:
Minister to abused and at-risk children.

Salem First partners with other agencies to provide a service for children of the community who are at risk of neglect and abuse.

The service is in response to the community's need. In a two-county area that includes Salem, there were six deaths and 754 confirmed cases of child abuse and neglect during 1996.

Called Family Building Blocks, the service is replicating The Relief Nursery, a nationally recognized child abuse prevention program that's been operating for more than two decades.

Goals of the free service are to reduce childabuse and neglect, decrease the number of children requiring foster care, help parents become and remain clean and sober, and support parents to secure and maintain adequate employment and housing.

"Very intensive child care is going on," Jane says. "The interventionists are doing therapeutic work with the children and their parents. They are also teaching parenting classes and making referrals for drug and alcohol recovery and anger and stress management. We have 24-hour emergency respite care for crisis situations involving young children."

She says most people who use the service come through state agencies, but a few are self-referred. "Since there's usually one teacher or therapist for every child, we only have 32 children in the program at one time. Unfortunately, we have a huge waiting list."

6.

Aldersgate United Methodist Church
ALEXANDRIA, VIRGINIA

To help children grow as disciples, Aldersgate Church has a comprehensive Christian education ministry directed by Ann Davis.

Here are a few of their models for ministry that Ann says are helping children grow as disciples.

Model 45:
Special events throughout the year nurture growth.

At least six times a year, Aldersgate offers a special event designed for children ages three years through kindergarten. Centered around a biblical story, they include games, crafts, and refreshments. An example: Noah's ark costume party.

Aldersgate has a special event at least six times a year for children in the first and second grades. At one event, called A Movie Critic's Afternoon, they discussed movies and rated them according to biblical guidelines. Then they entered rooms that had been transformed into theaters (complete with a refreshment stand with popcorn, soda, and candy) to watch movies. In another event, A Creation Party, children did scientific experiments to help them understand God's creation and presence in their lives.

Every Thursday morning in July, there's a Bible camp for children ages three years through kindergarten. It features games, crafts, and recreational activities centered around a special theme.

Children in third through sixth grades participate in a Covenant Discipleship group that meets weekly during Lent, focusing on works of caring (acts of kindness and justice) and works of faith (acts of devotion and worship).

Model 46:
Worship services recognize children and youth.

Aldersgate celebrates children and youth in worship services highlighting their gifts and talents. "Celebrate the Little Ones" recognizes all the children born and baptized during the year. A "Children's Sabbath" highlights current issues concerning children. Children assist in at least one worship service each year, participating as ushers, greeters, and lay readers. Youth plan and lead at least one worship service during the year.

Model 47:

Children and youth drama groups perform.

Parable Players—a drama group for children in third through sixth grades—perform frequently during worship services, church dinners, and other special events. Their performance of the story *Miss Tizzy* was presented at the Virginia Annual Conference in 1997 during a worship service on the Children's Initiative.

Aldersgate Youthworks!—a drama group for grades seven through twelve—has four to six large productions each year, and also performs scenes for worship services, church dinners, and other special events. The performances are on the stage with technical and musical support.

7.

Saint James United Methodist Church
ALBUQUERQUE, NEW MEXICO

"We are not training children to be Christians when they grow up. We are training them to be Christians now. They don't have to wait until they go through confirmation class or even until they start going to school.

"That's the foundation on which children's ministries are built at Saint James," says Judy Williamson, director of children's ministries for the 2,000-member congregation.

In addition to a creative church school that provides options for up to three hours of study, worship, and other activities every Sunday morning, Saint James has a comprehensive weekday ministry with children. "Every part of our children's ministry is designed to be a learning opportunity to help kids grow as disciples of Jesus Christ, and all the parts fit together."

Here are a few of Saint James' models for children's ministry:

Model 48:
Children write devotionals for the congregation.

Children write devotionals based on the Scriptures the minister uses as sermon texts during Advent and Lent. The devotionals are printed and made available for families to use as guides for worship in their homes.

"Our kids insights often amaze us," says Judy. "Writing the devotionals gives them a meaningful way to participate in the life of our church."

Model 49:
Vacation Bible school seeks to reach as many children as possible.

"We realize that families have different lifestyles and different travel schedules and that children have different interests and activities," says Judy. "So to reach as many children as possible, we provide options that make vacation Bible school as appealing and as easy to attend as possible."

In June, VBS is offered in the morning; in July, it is offered in the evening. Classes are for children from age two through the grade five. Older children help with worship and other activities.

To reach more children in the community, last year VBS volunteers took flyers advertising the VBS to about 600 homes in three carefully chosen neighborhoods. Several children came as a result of this promotional effort, Judy reports. In addition, she says, it helped establish the church's presence in the area and demonstrated the church's concern for children.

Model 50:
Church helps children develop strong prayer life.

To help children learn what prayer is, what prayer is not, and how to develop a meaningful prayer life, Saint James has a Pray and Play Day.

"This usually attracts children of families who are already involved in our church," Judy points out. "They are ready for another level of Christian experience. We show them the prayer board in the office where we post requests for prayer. And we show them how to submit requests to our prayer chain."

What impact does being involved in the prayer training have on the children? Judy shares this story: When a Saint James child was in a car accident, Judy took a group of children to visit her in the hospital. "Our presence seemed to bother her," Judy said. "I was afraid we might be doing more harm than good. We made it clear that we were praying for her. When she got out of the hospital and came back to church, we showed her the prayer board where her name had been listed. She gave no reaction. I didn't know what she was thinking or feeling. Months passed. Then one day I found a note taped to my office door. It said, 'Judy, my friend in Brownies, broke her leg. Can we pray for her?'"

Model 51:
Children learn about Christian symbols.

On four Wednesdays each year, Saint James preschoolers-usually accompanied by their mothers-visit the sanctuary. "We look at one of the stained-glass windows and learn the story behind it," says Judy. "We also invite the children to ask questions about anything in the sanctuary they may be curious about. As you can imagine, they sometimes have interesting questions. Then we have refreshments. While kids play, their mothers and I visit out on the playground. The kids are making friends and having fun. And so are the moms and I."

Model 52:
Children learn etiquette.

Ever heard of a church teaching children etiquette? Saint James does. "We think the church needs to help children learn to relate to others with attitudes and actions that flow from genuine respect and concern for all God's children," says Judy. "And that's the purpose of our etiquette class."

Judy teaches the children how to introduce themselves to strangers and how to relate with others in a variety of settings, including worship, weddings, and social events. She says the class is just as popular with boys as it is with girls and parents.

"We go to the mall and look at formals and tuxedoes and silverware. And we have lunch at a fancy restaurant and practice good table manners," says Judy. "Sometimes we sponsor a tea for the parents and other adults of the church. Children make the tea and pour it."

Model 53:
Children lead worship.

On a Sunday in October, children lead worship in all three services, Judy reports. "Everything relates to the theme of the minister's sermon. Our children's orchestra plays, our children's choir sings, our children's puppet club performs. Our children's theater group gives a skit. We light candles to remember children who are disabled, who are being abused, who are living in poverty, who are receiving little spiritual nurture, and who are facing other obstacles."

On a weekend afternoon before Thanksgiving, children come to the church and make items their families can use to enrich their worship at home around the theme for Christmas.

At four o'clock on Christmas Eve, children lead a worship service at the church that's designed primarily for children but also attracts numerous adults. "We never rehearse this service," says Judy. "We encourage the kids to be sincere and natural. And to relax. They have enough pressure in their lives these days without the church adding to it by demanding that they put on a perfect performance."

Model 54:
Children create cards to show they care.

Saint James' people who have special joys or concern are listed on a board in the church office. Children—individually or as Sunday school classes or other groups—take a look at the board regularly, then create cards especially for them, with appropriate greetings and drawings. The cards are delivered by ministers and laypeople who visit.

Model 55:
Church carefully selects and trains workers.

"We encourage teachers to work as teams," Judy says. "Some people think team teaching means you teach this Sunday and I'll teach next. But by team teaching, we mean two people in the classroom every Sunday, working together as a team. This is good for the teachers, and it's good for the children."

To minimize the risk of children being abused or otherwise endangered by church staff or volunteers, Saint James takes several precautions according to Judy.

"We don't accept people as teachers until they have been active in our church for at least six months. We carefully screen all workers in the children's ministry. Our preschool and nursery workers are fingerprinted and we do FBI checks on them."

Model 56:
Dinner helps different classrooms users communicate.

"My globe is missing!" "The Scouts have messed up my room again!" Ever hear complaints like those? Saint James has a model that's reducing such conflicts.

"Something is happening every day at Saint James, not just on Sundays," Judy explains. "Many of our classrooms are used by several different groups. We invite everyone who uses our building to a dinner where we celebrate all of our programs and activities, and emphasize how each fits into our mission."

To help people who use the same room get acquainted, during the celebration they are assigned seats at the same table. They talk with one another about what they and their groups are doing and why they are doing it. Mutual respect and appreciation grows. They become more aware that the room and what's in it is not their exclusive property—that they are sharing space with others who are equally committed to equally vital ministries. Consequently, they become more patient with each other.

"We suggest that people who use the same room exchange phone numbers, and call one another if something in the room they use is messed up or missing," Judy says "It works."

8.

Saint Luke's United Methodist Church
OKLAHOMA CITY, OKLAHOMA

"Our goal is to help children experience God's love and to learn to share God's love with others," says Marcia Turner, director of the Children's Division at Saint Luke's.

A variety of models for ministry helps Saint Luke's children experience and share God's love, and thereby grow as disciples. Here are a few of them:

Model 57:
Children have adult prayer partners.

Each child age four through the fifth grade is partnered with an adult from the congregation who has volunteered to be a prayer partner with a child.

In January, the child and his or her adult partner meet at a reception. While they drink lemonade and eat cookies, they exchange information sheets that include their addresses, telephone numbers, birthdays, and special interests.

"The only requirement for our prayer partners is that they pray every day for each other," says Marcia. "They agree not to give gifts to each other, but they can exchange birthday and Christmas cards."

Marcia says the prayer partner ministry is having a positive impact on the children and the adults. "Among other things," she says, "it's building meaningful relationships between generations. In a large church like ours, we think it's vitally important to integrate generations as much as possible and to help people get acquainted."

Model 58:
Pastors teach children about Communion.

Several times a year, Saint Luke's has a children's Communion service. Children and their parents gather in a chapel with one of the pastors, who explains what Communion means to United Methodists, replies to any questions, and then serves Communion.

"Our intent is to help our children become comfortable with the Communion ritual," Marcia says. "Our parents and our children love this informal time of worship."

Model 59:
Butterflies teach children about new beginnings.

Nearly a month before Easter, Marcia's office at Saint Luke's becomes a butterfly hatchery. That's when she receives larvae that she and the children of the church care for until the larvae transform into butterflies. "We release the butterflies on Easter morning to symbolize the new beginnings that God gives us," Marcia explains. "Adults and kids stand on our church steps and watch the butterflies begin their journeys." Children's classes reflect on the transformation they have seen, and what it says about changes that occur in each person's life.

Model 60:
Children motivate adults to support missions.

The children's division recently sponsored a mission project to collect teddy bears to give to the police, fire, and ambulance personnel so they could pass them on to children in crisis.

"We collected bears for several weeks, then on Promotion Sunday, we had a teddy bear picnic as an all-church lunch after worship," Marcia says. "We put the more than 350 bears we had received at the bears' own table. It was fun for kids and adults."

On Super Bowl Sunday every year, the children station themselves around the church with soup kettles to collect pocket change from the congregation. They collected $867 in 1998 and gave it to the food pantry at the McKee Center, a component of Skyline (United Methodist) Ministries, which assists people in Oklahoma City who are having financial emergencies.

Model 61:
The Children's Division sponsors a children's carnival.

After worship on the first Sunday in May, Saint Luke's has an outdoor spring carnival for children. "Our parking lot is transformed into a carnival atmosphere," Marcia says. "We have a cook wagon where we make hot dogs and hamburgers, we have pony rides, lots of games, and a children's book fair. We sponsor a tea for mothers and grandmothers on Mother's Day."

9.

First United Methodist Church
Baton Rouge, Louisiana

Model 62:
Day camp helps children spread God's love.

First Church in Baton Rouge provides a hands-on mission experience for children that's teaching them they can spread God's love.

Their Mission Day Camp is a Monday through Friday learning-serving experience during a week in the summer for children who are going into the fifth, sixth, and seventh grades.

"Each day we study God's word and what it means to serve and be in mission," says Charlotte Naper, director of children's ministries. "Then we go out into the community the rest of the day and serve. We limit enrollment to twenty because that's all the room we have for people at some places we serve."

Here's the schedule the Mission Day Camp followed during the summer of 1998, as described by Charlotte:

"Monday, we came to the church and talked about what it means to be in mission for Christ, and we learned about journaling, which the children did throughout the week. The children wrote Scripture passages and other good thoughts on about fifty colored index cards and decorated them with markers. We got them ready for our mission trip on Friday to a nursing home.

"Tuesday, we went to a soup kitchen. Our kids served food, bussed tables, and helped any what they could.

"Wednesday, we went to Saeger-Brown-the United Methodist Committee on Relief depot in Baldwin, Louisiana, where we ship mission supplies all over the world. After touring the depot, the children put school kits together for children in another country and helped with some other projects. They saw what our United Methodist Church does and what it means to the world.

"Thursday, we went to an inner-city ministry and took treat bags to the seventy-five kids who attend the mission. We gave a party, sang, and served refreshments.

"Friday, we went to a nursing home, sang for the residents, and took them the little cards with the Scripture verses and positive thoughts that the kids had made on Monday."

Charlotte says the kids are encouraged to think about the mission they are doing and to reflect about the people they are serving, what life is like for them, how they must feel. "The week has a powerful impact on our children," she concludes.

Model 63:
Children's classes support mission projects.

At First Church there's a strong mission emphasis in all the children's classes, Charlotte explains. Each third- through fifth-grade class supports a mission project throughout the year. An example: the fifth-grade class, taught by Kathryn Moore, secretary to the Louisiana Area bishop, collected $1,290 in pennies and sent the money to foreign missions. How did they collect such a large amount? In September, kids from the class went to adult Sunday school classes, appealed for support of missions, and left a big jar in the class for people to drop pennies in each week. In May, the classes turned in their pennies.

Model 64:
Children at Tulsa church adopt missionaries.

Another model for helping children grow as disciples by being part of the church's mission efforts is used at Boston Avenue United Methodist Church in Tulsa, Oklahoma. The Reverend EvaMarie Herndon Campbell, coordinator of children's ministries, says each children's class adopts a missionary. They also learn about the work done by their church's Volunteers-in-Mission teams and make gifts for teams to take on mission trips. They also go to mission agencies in Tulsa and learn about the needs of people served by the agencies, how the agencies help people, and how their class and their church can help the agencies.

10.

First United Methodist Church
TULSA, OKLAHOMA

Model 65:
Even babies go to Sunday school.

Baby's Bible Class at First Church is designed for infants, toddlers, and two year olds. Students are seated around a low U-shaped table- babies are in carseat-type chairs, toddlers are in miniature director's chairs. The teacher sits on the floor inside the U.

"Our mission is to make disciples for Jesus Christ of all children," says the Reverend Connie Ichord, the church's minister of education. "We begin teaching children about God's great love while they are still infants. Through simple songs, pictures and toys, they receive affirmation of God's love."

Connie says Christian messages are underscored by teaching methods based on how babies learn. "Each lesson takes ten to fifteen minutes and is fast paced to hold the children's short attention spans. With simple songs, our babies are taught about God's creation, God's love, God's Word, God's families, and God's Son. Miniature Bibles, figures of families, and animals are some of the tools we use for the children to see and touch."

Parents of babies are given beepers, so they can be contacted quickly if their child needs them.

When children are two years old, their curriculum reinforces the same Bible story of God's love. Scripture pictures produced by Tulsa First are used to help the kids grasp ideas.

Baby's Bible Class is just the beginning. When children turn three, they go to Preschool Church. "They begin praising God with active songs that lead into worship and the Lord's Prayer," Connie says. "The storyteller animates the Bible story. We walk slowly through the Bible from Genesis to Revelation."

Children's Church is the next step. "We teach the kids the who, where, when, and what of the Bible. Puppets introduce the lesson and teaching. Our kids learn about praise, prayer, worship, and salvation as we focus on Christ."

Babies Bible Class began at Tulsa First fourteen years ago, Connie says. "We have probably had 2,000 children take part in it. Our families value this ministry."

Model 66:

Texas church has classes for infants and toddlers.

A Sunday school class at University United Methodist Church in San Antonio, Texas, teaches infants and toddlers (up to 24 months) about God's love through repetitive songs, finger plays, stuffed animals, and sounds. "By the time they enter the class for 3 year olds, these kids get it," says Shari Stephens of University Church, a church that has more than 500 children every Sunday.

11.

Saint Marks United Methodist Church
PENSACOLA, FLORIDA

Model 67:
New baby ministry gives tender loving care.

"Expectant mothers are special to our congregation, and we let them know it," says Esther Felt of Saint Mark's. She directs her church's Heaven Sent/New Baby Ministry.

"We give a book to every expectant mother who is a member of our church or has visited a few times," Esther explains. "Right now we are giving a mother's journal that we buy from Cokesbury. It has space for the expectant mom to jot down her thoughts and feelings each week, and Scriptures for her to read.

"The day the baby is born, we put a ribbon on their mail box. When the mom and baby come home from the hospital, we take the family a meal for that first night. A few days later, we bring the mom a present-usually some bubble bath, just something to pamper her a little."

In December, all the babies born to Saint Mark's families during the year receive a special invitation to come to church, Esther says. "We give the mom a Christmas tree ornament that a member of our church has made. On one side we have printed 'Saint Mark United Methodist Church,' and on the other side we've printed the baby's name and the birthdate."

Esther says the moms and dads really appreciate these expressions of love and support.

Part Three

Ministering to and with Children in the Community

12.

Trinity United Methodist Church
ALBANY, NEW YORK

Model 68:
Buddy program is for children with HIV/AIDS.

Trinity Church sponsors a Buddy Program for children infected by or affected by HIV/AIDS. Nancirose Halse, coordinator of the program, says this model ministry is brightening the lives of youth and adults, as well as the children it serves.

"In 1995, I was taking a class at seminary on social ministry and my paper was to be on The United Methodist Church's approach to AIDS," Nancirose said, filling me in on how the Buddy Program began.

"When I asked the General Board of Global Ministries for help, they sent me a packet of information on fund grants for projects for persons with AIDS or HIV. I brought this to the attention of the senior pastor at Trinity. We knew people in our area needed help and began thinking about a project."

At that time, Nancirose was a volunteer chaplain at Albany Medical Center-the regional AIDS treatment center. She spoke with a social worker there for mothers and children with AIDS or HIV. The social worker told her the hospital had been trying for three years to start a program for children infected or affected by HIV. They wanted to link these children up one-on-one with a teenage buddy for at least one afternoon a month.

Nancirose explains that children with AIDS/HIV often experience alienation and isolation. The program the social worker had in mind would address these problems by providing the children with teenage buddies. The obstacle delaying the program was recruiting and training the teenagers.

Nancirose learned that Albany County Health Department already had an outreach program with teenagers called TOUCH: Teens Outreach For

Persons with AIDS. They were looking for a project. With Nancirose's help, they quickly found one.

Trinity's congregation was enthusiastic about working with the Albany Medical Center and the Albany County Health Department in developing the Buddy Program ministry. "We have an older church," Nancirose said. "The majority of our active members have children who are already grown, so they were eager to do something for children but just didn't exactly know how to go about it. This was the answer we had been looking for."

With the pastor's help, Nancirose wrote a proposal, sent it to the United Methodist General Board of Global Ministries, and soon received a grant, with the understanding that it would be matched by work and space of equal value.

A letter from Trinity and the Albany County HIV/AIDS Task Force was sent to parents of children who might profit from this ministry. It pointed out that the Buddy program was being designed to offer recreational activities and outings, not therapy.

Parents welcomed the invitation. "Our ministry has been successful from the very beginning," says Nancirose. "Twenty children are registered with the program, and attendance averages sixteen to eighteen children each time. We could have a lot more, but we limit the number so we can provide the best of care."

The boys and girls are black, white, and Hispanic. They are in various stages of HIV/AIDS or live in family situations with a member or members who have HIV/AIDS. Most are from disproportionately lower-income families. Their teenage buddies come from four high schools in the area, and are also from disproportionately lower-income families.

The Buddy Program at Trinity meets throughout the year on the third Saturday afternoon each month from one o'clock until four o'clock. Two vans from the church, driven by church volunteers, transport the children to and from church and other locations, such as museums, parks, and swimming pools.

"In each van, we have emergency kits with gloves and preparations for a medical emergency," says Nancirose. "We don't administer medicine, but we make sure that diets are appropriate. Part of the grant money gives a healthy snack at each meeting."

Teenagers take turns riding with drivers on the routes. When they arrive at a home, the teenager goes to the door and accompanies the child to the van. They also help with discipline when it is necessary.

"Our teens are incredibly faithful," says Nancirose. "When there's an event like going to the amusement park, the teenagers outnumber the children. They go with them everywhere. One time they went apple picking.

They were giving the little one's piggyback rides, and just having a great time."

The teens not only come the third Saturday of each month to be with the children, they also meet every two weeks for training, which includes basic-first aid and child activity planning.

At the beginning of the Buddy Program, the teens participated in an eight-hour workshop led by a medical social worker from the Albany Medical Center and other professionals from the health department. Subjects they have studied include stages of child development, appropriate activities, child proofing a room, children living with HIV (a video), importance of confidentiality, and how HIV may affect a child's development.

The teens also help support the Buddy Program by having car washes, AIDS walks, and other fund raisers.

"Our children like the Saturday afternoon activities so much they would like to come more often than once a month," says Nancirose. "By now the kids know one another. Some of them feel like talking with one another. Others don't. We have one little boy who usually curls up and sucks his thumb, and goes to sleep on the way home. They aren't under any pressure from us. There's no testing, no grading. Just positive reinforcement."

When the children turn thirteen and are too old for the program, most of them want to stay. "It's really hard to tell them they can't," said Nancirose. "We just don't have the person power to extended the program."

People in Albany have become aware of the Buddy Program, and some benefactors have underwritten special events, such as Christmas and Easter parties.

Model 69:
The church works closely with other organizations.

One lesson we can learn by examining this model is that a church doesn't have to provide all the pieces to a ministry. You can work with other organizations in your community who also want to help but can't do the job alone.

13.

Boston Avenue United Methodist Church
TULSA, OKLAHOMA

Model 70:
Respite helps children and parents.

Children with disabilities come to Boston Avenue Church two Friday evenings every month. They arrive as early as six thirty and stay until eleven o'clock.

While the kids are having fun together—doing arts and crafts, playing games, watching videos—their parents are free to do whatever they need to do, says Becky Price, who directs younger children programs at Boston Avenue. Some go shopping, others go to dinner and a movie. A few stay home and work on projects or just relax.

The number of children who come varies from ten to fifteen. "We limit the number so we can serve the kids adequately," says Becky. "Some are toddlers and others are in their late teens, but are more like six-year-olds developmentally.

"When parents apply for their child to be part of the respite ministry, we review the child's handicapping conditions to determine if we are able to care for him or her properly. Several have been coming for years. We know them and their parents well," Becky says.

The respite is staffed by volunteers and by paid workers.

Boston Avenue has provided this ministry for more than a decade. It's available for anyone in the community. And there's no charge.

Operating costs are covered by the church budget and by a Sunday school class.

14.

Saint Mark United Methodist Church
MONTGOMERY, ALABAMA

Model 71:

Church hosts school for children with special needs.

Prior to 1996, not much happened during weekdays at Saint Mark Church, a 250-member congregation.

"Now good things are going on around here every day, and I am pleased," declares Mark LaBranche, the pastor.

What's going on?

Saint Marks is host of Churchill Academy, a school for children who would have difficulty learning in a regular school setting. Sixty children attend classes from kindergarten through the eighth grade that are designed specifically for them. Their diagnoses range from attention deficit disorder to learning disabled to gifted.

Mark says that even though the kids vary in their areas of strengths and weaknesses, all need a supportive environment and individualized academic programming that teaches to their strengths, addresses their weaknesses, and encourages strategies for compensation.

Churchill Academy teachers are special education specialists. There's at least one teacher for every ten students, and teachers are assisted by trained volunteers.

Mark says making their church building available for a ministry has not only benefited the students and the community at large. It has also helped the church.

"We see Churchill Academy as a mission of the church," he says. "I can't point to statistics that show the school has contributed to the numerical growth that we are experiencing, but I am confident that it has contributed to the growth of our outlook and our mission. That's vitally important!"

15.

First United Methodist Church
PONCA CITY, OKLAHOMA

Police officers in Ponca City, Oklahoma carry bunny dolls in their patrol cars. Captain Jerry Neville tells why.

"We give the bunnies to children caught between parents during domestic disturbances, and during investigations of abuse and neglect, and even when we're making contacts with children who are just plain impoverished."

Captain Neville explains that during domestic abuse cases the children often feel unloved and very insecure. "Their focus often goes immediately from their parents' problems to their bunny." He says the bunnies help "break the ice" when investigators are preparing to question a child. "We've even used the bunnies during interviews of sexual abuse by allowing the child to show where or how he or she was touched."

Bunnies are also used by the Domestic Violence Program of North Central Oklahoma. Christy Williams, director, says many of the children they serve have been exposed to violence between their parents and many have experienced violence firsthand.

"The children arrive at our facility frightened, confused and insecure," says Williams. "During the first contact with them, our staff counselors give them bunnies to keep. Children find these bunnies to be an unconditional receptor of their affection. What is especially touching is to see children who unfortunately have to return to the shelter for a second time and they come clutching their bunnies close to their chests."

Williams says the bunnies are much more than a toy. "They assure the child that someone cares for him."

Model 72:
The church works with "Bunny Lady."

Where do the bunnies used by the police department and domestic violence center come from? First United Methodist Church provides them.

The bunny program began in May 1992 when a member of First Church—Jane Storrusten, who's now affectionately called "Bunny Lady"—was making a floppy-eared bunny for her grandchildren. While she worked, Jane thought about her own childhood. Painful memories of abuse and neglect surfaced. Rather than focus on the abuse she had experienced, Jane focused on children who were experiencing abuse that very day in her hometown. It wasn't too late to help them.

A few days later, Jane drove to the Ponca City police station. Her old fears of people in authority and of being rejected were so strong she couldn't get out of her car. Officer Jerry Neville drove up and parked right beside her. Hardly realizing what she was doing, Jane burst out of her car, thrust an armful of bunnies at Jerry, and asked if he could see that they reached abused children. He said yes. And he said yes again when Jane asked him if he could use more bunnies.

What began as Jane's personal ministry quickly grew, and she invited friends at her church to help. In 1996, the New Beginnings Sunday School Class started giving $50 each month toward the cost of materials. Friends joined Jane in stitching, dressing, and stuffing the bunny bodies.

In 1997, with Jane's approval and encouragement, the Missions and Social Concerns Work Area at First Church adopted the Bunny Program as a ministry.

Before bunnies are distributed, the pastor, Denny Hook, leads a service of blessing for children who will received them.

Bunnies produced by First Church are now used by the Kay County Child Welfare offices. "Each bunny comes to us with a lot of love put into them," says Andrea Gifford, a social worker there. "Children seem to pick out the bunny that best portrays themselves or how they are feeling. We have seen them take the bunnies to court with them, acting as if the bunny was their only friend. The bunnies seem to fill a gap, not only for the children, but also for the social workers who get to give them to the children. To be able to do a kindness for the child during these stressful times is a blessing to all us who are involved."

For more information about the bunny program, write First United Methodist Church,, 200 S. Sixth, Ponca City, OK 74601. Phone (580)762-1681.

16.

Southern Hills United Methodist Church
OKLAHOMA CITY, OKLAHOMA

A United Methodist News Service article about the Oklahoma City federal building bombing in 1995 mentioned that Southern Hills Church in Oklahoma City was offering to receive expressions of concern people wanted to pass along to survivors, families of victims, and others involved in the bombing.

Model 73:
Children's classes send cards to disaster victims.

During the next few weeks Southern Hills received more than a thousand cards and letters. Many were from children in Sunday school classes all across the nation.

Before me is a copy of a note received in a packet from a church in Iowa. Written by an 11-year-old child, it is addressed to "a rescue worker." It says: "On every news broadcast there's something about the bombing. I watched you risk your life trying to rescue people who were trapped. I appreciate all you have done. You are heroes because you help others."

Cards like this comforted many people in their times of loss. The children say writing them helped them express their concern and helped them feel they had done something to help.

Incidentally, the secretary at Southern Hills asked her mother to help her read the cards. The next day, her mother said, "You know, after reading what these kids have written, I'm not as worried about the future."

What the Iowa church did is a good model for children's Sunday school classes. When there's a disaster, the class might give students a few minutes in class to write notes expressing their concern in their own words. And, to personalize their notes, they might enclose their pictures. The teacher could then send the notes to a United Methodist church in the area, requesting that they pass along the notes. How do you find the address of a United Methodist church in the area? Call 1-800-874-3211.

Model 74:
Church distributes children's cards.

What Southern Hills did is a good model for churches to follow when there is a major disaster in the area. Let the United Methodist News Service know that your church is serving as a "clearinghouse for caring," receiving expressions of concern and passing them along to those who have experienced losses.

17.

Asbury United Methodist Church
TULSA, OKLAHOMA

Back in 1996, Mary Randolph, director of Single Adult Ministries at Asbury Church, was concerned about a member of the church whose wife had died of cancer.

When Mary invited him to a Single Adult Ministries activity, he thanked her for her concern, but told her that his five children needed help dealing with the death of their mother even more than he did.

Model 75:
Asbury helps children cope with grief.

Mary searched for ways her church might help children cope with grief. Her search led Asbury UMC to becoming affiliate with Rainbows for All God's Children, a national support group for children experiencing grief.

Asbury's Rainbow ministry is directed by Jill Glenn, a clinical therapist who has received Rainbow's certification and is Rainbow's director for the Tulsa region. She points out that death isn't the only loss that can cause grief to children. Moving to a new city, a divorce, or any other painful loss can lead to feelings of grief, guilt, low self-esteem, and anger.

"It's difficult for parents and children to deal with grief by themselves," says Jill. "They each have their own issues to work on."

She explains that grieving is a process that sometimes takes years. "As you grow up, you don't suddenly lose those feelings."

To help children work through their grief, the Rainbow program offers a session each week for fourteen weeks. Each session lasts forty-five minutes. Students are broken into small groups according to their year in school and each group has a facilitator Jill has trained to lead the discussion.

"We talk a lot about self-esteem and help the children realize that it's okay for them to be angry," Jill said. "They are promised that anything said during the group is confidential, so all can feel free to talk openly about their feelings."

Jill says Rainbows is not a counseling session or therapy for the children. "It's strictly a peer support group with caring, trained adults to guide them. Our aim is to implant in these grieving children a belief in their own goodness and a belief that each change in life can become an occasion for a new beginning."

Parents visit once for an orientation and twice for "Celebrate Me" sessions during the fourteen weeks. Positive Parenting training is also available through Rainbows.

For more information about Rainbows, Jill Glenn invites you to call her in Tulsa at (918)622-7373.

Related Models From Other Churches

Model 76:

Little Rock church ministers to children of divorce.

Saint James United Methodist Church in Little Rock, Arkansas has an extensive ministry to children whose parents have recently divorced. It is developed by Jenni Douglas Duncan. In addition to serving as children's coordinator at Saint James, Jennie leads workshops on caring for children, and she's written a book published by Discipleship Resources that contains activities and sessions for helping children. To contact Jenni, call (501)225-7372 or (501)455-1432.

Model 77:

Florida church offers recovery program for children.

First United Methodist Church in Niceville, Florida offers a divorce recovery program for children and teenagers who are having difficulty accepting and dealing with the divorce of their parents. The programs last eight weeks and are held twice a year in September and February.

Model 78:

Oklahoma church has support group for stepparents

When Dan Peil, pastor of New Hope United Methodist Church in Oklahoma City, Oklahoma realized that he and his wife, Marilyn, were far from being the only stepparents in his congregation, he helped develop the Step Parents Support Group. "We share ways that help us be better parents and build healthier relationships," says Peil, "And we are there for one another."

18.

Ministry to Children of Prisoners
OKLAHOMA CONFERENCE

Our nation's more than 1.1 million prisoners have tens of thousands of minor children. Their children—like all other children—are unique individuals. We must be hesitant to make generalizations about them, as if they were all alike. Yet many children of prisoners have similar backgrounds and needs.

For example, many have experienced violence in their homes. And often alcohol or some other drug has been involved. Not only have they witnessed verbal and physical fights between their parents, they also have sustained emotional, physical, sexual, and other forms of abuse from their mothers, fathers, siblings, other relatives, and other caregivers.

Most children of prisoners have frequently been shunned, whispered about, called degrading names, and mistreated in various other ways by kids and by adults as well. Many have been told they are no good so many times they are convinced they are worthless. Some have become emotionally numb in order to survive.

Many children of prisoners have witnessed their parents being arrested. Some have encountered other traumatic situations where a friend was killed or their own lives were in danger from drive-by shootings or some other form of violence

While some children of prisoners experience a middle- or upper-income lifestyle, many more live in households with family incomes below the poverty line. The parent who is not in prison is in financial bondage, struggling to pay for food, clothing, shelter, and other essentials.

Many children of prisoners eventually go to prison. In fact, some experts say kids with mothers or fathers in prison are at least three times more likely than other kids to be incarcerated at some time in their lives.

Model 79:
Prisoners' children go to camp.

Stan Basler, director of Criminal Justice and Mercy Ministries of the Oklahoma Conference of The United Methodist Church, says children of prisoners are often the forgotten victims of crime.

For the past four summers, the Oklahoma Conference has sponsored a weeklong camp for boys and girls between the ages of eight and fourteen who have a parent—or both parents—in prison. It's called New Day Camp.

Last year, approximately 100 kids from across the state came to the United Methodist Cross Point Camp on Lake Texoma in southeast Oklahoma. The children were recommended for the camp by relatives, public school teachers, counselors, social workers, and pastors.

Sixty-five volunteer counselors—carefully chosen and trained—worked with the campers. Together, they played softball, volleyball, basketball, and table games. They swam and went for rides in canoes. They did crafts, including painting, woodworking, and sculpture. Sixteen of the older kids took on and successfully completed the camp's ropes challenge course that is designed to teach cooperation, teamwork, and goals achievement.

But the camp was more than fun and games, says Basler. "In this peaceful setting, the kids were far away from drive-by shootings, which many of them frequently witness. Since caring adults were in charge, they were given a break from heavy responsibilities. They didn't have to cook, clean house, take care of siblings, stop fights. They could be children-act their age."

Basler says one goal for New Day Camp is to bring kids with similar backgrounds together in a safe place where they can share their feelings about their incarcerated parents and gain insights from one another that will help them cope.

"It's a place where children don't need to be ashamed or hide the fact that they have a parent in prison," he says. "They can find friendship and peer intimacy that they seldom experience on the school playground. They receive love, acceptance, modeling and compassion from adults—male and female, young and old."

In focus groups, kids have opportunities to talk about what's going on in their lives and to express their deepest feelings. Hearing each other talk helps them discover that others carry burdens much like theirs. Right away, they begin to feel connected with one another.

Feeling connected with other people is difficult for many of the kids back in their own community. One teenager said, "I don't want to share my business at home because other kids will tease me and talk about me." Some said they were also afraid to share their feelings with their parents because they were usually near the emotional breaking point. Others talked about having to care for parents who weren't coping well.

Several campers said they felt torn in their family systems. They wanted to stay loyal to the incarcerated parent but they also wanted to get along with family members who were angry with the person who was in prison. Others had new relationships in the family—such as stepparents—and were often told by them and by others how bad their incarcerated parent was.

One nine-year-old girl told about her best friend being raped, murdered, and put in a dumpster near her apartment. All the children in one group raised their hands when asked if they have lost friends because of car accidents, shootings, or suicides. They know what death means, but they are not so sure what life means.

On the last day of camp, the kids developed their own personal peace plan. They were given a card, and on it they wrote where their place of peace was to be, and the name of a person in their life who might help provide peace for them. They laminated their cards and took them home. When they get in tough situations they are advised to pull out the card and review the plan they have developed.

Resurrection Church in Oklahoma City—a church for prisoners and their families—has developed a special ministry for children of prisoners. For more information, call the Reverend Dale Tremper: (405)528-0963.

19.

Hobson United Methodist Church
NASHVILLE, TENNESSEE

When I asked the Reverend Janet Wolf what her church—Hobson—does for children, she replied, "It's hard to answer that question because the children have done so much for us."

During the 1950s, before the neighborhood changed dramatically, Hobson had more than 1,700 members. When Janet arrived in 1993, she could only count on having thirty people in worship-only one of whom was under sixty-five. "We had no families with children," Janet recalls. "We had a huge building but no money. Some members didn't think Hobson could afford a full-time pastor."

Today the community around Hobson is even more diverse than it was when she arrived. Many refugee families from all over the world have moved in. At the elementary school nearest the church, children speak twenty-six languages.

In the midst of diversity and poverty, Hobson is seeking to welcome, include, and empower everyone, regardless of age, gender, family, race/ethnicity, economic circumstances, or sexual orientation, for mission and ministry through Jesus Christ. More than fifty children and youth are now involved in the church, and fifty more take part in its various community ministries. The church is very much alive and filled with hope and joy.

Model 80:
Rebuilding starts with Bible study.

"The way we started rebuilding was to go back to Bible study and deal with biblical images of the church," explains Janet, a graduate of Vanderbilt University Divinity School. "At one time we had about thirty images we were working with, but we finally settled on four that became most important."

The first biblical image adopted was—*We are Pentecost people.* Janet explains: "This image—based on Acts 2—gave us hope because God's spirit falls on everybody, and when the spirit falls, folks spill out to the streets, and suddenly all people hear in their own language. So we started wondering: What would it mean if we spoke the language of kids on the street, or prostitutes, or drug dealers? What would it mean if God's spirit gave us the wisdom and courage and power to speak in the language that other folks understand as their own language?"

The second biblical image—We are ambassadors of reconciliation—is based on 2 Corinthians 5:14-20. Hobson's mission statement says: "In Christ Jesus, we are a new creation; the old has passed away so we no longer view anyone from the old human point of view. Reconciliation has already happened through Christ Jesus and we are to live it out, inviting others to be reconciled so that healing and justice happen; evangelism connects witness and justice, church and community."

The third biblical image—We are a community of hospitality and love—is based on John 3:16, Luke 14:12, Acts. 10, and Psalm 139:14. This image acknowledges that God loves all people, not just the church folks or the righteous or holy. Consequently, it affirms that Hobson people are to love everyone well and to be glad for differences and diversity.

Janet adds this observation: "Luke 14:12 reminds us that when we have a feast, we shouldn't just invite folks who can pay us back. Instead, we should invite folks from the street, who can't bring their own barbecued chicken."

Here's the fourth biblical image Hobson people chose to shape their lives—"We are to be persistent, passionate, creative, aggressive, risk-taking and sometimes outrageous disciples." It's based on Matthew 15:21-28, Mark 2:1-12, Luke 13:10-17, and John 4:1-42. Hobson's mission statement explains: "Everyone is to take part in mission and ministry, being the Body of Christ in and for the world. We will fall short and make mistakes, but we are called to trust in God's grace and mercy and 'Just do it!'"

Model 81:
Bible study shapes the church's identity and mission.

The four biblical images of the church that Hobson people adopted became their guidelines for making administrative decisions and designing new ministries.

Janet said, "Community Bible study is central to our identity and we do it Wednesdays, Sundays, and also in committee meetings. Our sermons come out of Wednesday night community Bible study so that by the time we get to worship a group of folks have already wrestled with what the text might mean for us. New partners-especially those from the streets, those struggling with addiction or mental illness, those coming out of prison, those in poverty, and those pushed to the margins-help us hear the Scripture in new ways. They have an urgency about what God is doing in the world. They are glad for the gospel good news that promises to turn the world upside down. It is this partnership with people in need—not just to and for people in need—that has defined Hobson."

Their understanding of what their church should be and do led Hobson to decide that the land they owned adjoining the church should be more than a vacant lot. It should be an extension of the church's ministry: proclaiming God's love, promoting reconciliation, helping people experience oneness in Christ.

And now the land is an extension of the church's ministry! On it, five houses now stand, providing comfortable homes for low-income families. Construction was a joint venture between Hobson and Habitat for Humanity.

Janet's years of experience as a community organizer helped her as Habitat and others brought together a diverse network of business, professional, community, and religious leaders. "Lots of people worked hard and dreamed large in order to join with God in what God was already doing," says Janet. "I, fortunately, was around for the celebration!"

Thanks to considerable media coverage, the housing project changed Hobson's image in the community and across Nashville. Janet knows that a good public image can help a church attract more people, but she values far more the impact the housing project had on the church's self-image.

"We had been so closed in on ourselves," she said. "And now we had let go of something we valued, land we had owned since 1865. We weren't using the land. It was just sitting there, but it was really hard to let go. Once we did let it go, and once we saw what God can do with a little bit, we realized what God might do if we really offered up all we had."

Janet says when the housing project got underway, kids from the neighborhood started showing up at the church.

"I think they came because we were outside hammering on those houses," Janet says. "All kinds of people were coming and going. It was exciting to see something new happening in this old neighborhood."

Model 82:
Church builds playground for community kids.

Hobson worked with others to build a joint playground between the new houses and the church. "Of course, the kids loved the playground," says Janet. "And they concluded that the people appearently cared about them."

One Sunday, in the middle of a worship service, a ten- year-old boy walked into the chapel, looked around at the congregation, and asked, "Is it okay to stay or what?" Several people spoke up, assuring him he was welcomed. The youngster sat down, and joined them in worship.

"After that, we started getting a number of children who had never been in church before." says Janet. "They got themselves up in the morning, showed up with no adult, just walked in, came and went on their own. Up until then, people were always silent during the service. All of a sudden we had these kids who were always speaking out. When we were in prayer, I would ask, 'For what are we thankful?' Before the kids came, there would always be utter silence. But these kids would just go on forever listing what they were grateful for: gum, trees, flowers, birds, a sister, shoes, even noodles they ate that morning. They'd keep shouting out what they were thankful for until I'd say, 'That's nice. We'll save some for next Sunday.'"

Janet says the congregation had asked her when she first arrived to pray for new members and especially for children. "I don't think they had these children or the other new members, mostly folks from the streets, in mind," she said, smiling.

Model 83:

Members pray for one another.

Every Sunday at Hobson, index cards are placed in the bulletin and people are invited to jot down on them their joys and concerns. The cards are picked up. At the end of the service, everyone is asked to take a card and to pray everyday during the week for the person whose card he or she has received.

"In the beginning, some adults were concerned that a child might get their prayer cards, but we soon discovered that the kids were far more serious about prayer than we had imagined," Janet says. "Kids who couldn't read asked someone what was on the card. Those who couldn't write, drew pictures."

One Sunday, a seven-year-old girl brought her prayer card to Janet. "She had drawn a picture of a boy on the ground with holes in him and blood running out of the holes, and a little girl was standing next to the body with tears streaming down her face," Janet said.

"She told us that the day before, she had been standing next to a sixteen year old in a housing project. He was gunned down and killed in a drug deal. So the little girl said, 'I want you to pray for my friend who died and for me who almost died and for all the kids who aren't dead yet.'"

Janet says that experience transformed the congregation's understanding prayer. "This little girl brought us her hardest hurt and believed prayer would make a difference. It just kept being one thing after another like that. The children totally disrupted and redefined our service and really taught us to be the church."

Model 84:

Children's committee listens to children.

When children began coming, the congregation concluded it was time to establish a children's committee, something Hobson hadn't needed in years since there had been no children.

"The first time our children's committee met, I went with several adults to our meeting room," Janet said. "A child was already there, sitting in this rocking chair. When she saw us she was puzzled and she said, 'I didn't know grow-ups come to the children's meeting.' None of us had a clue that children thought they should come, but they did come from the beginning. They reasoned that since it was a children's committee meeting, then children were supposed to be there."

Model 85:

Children's ministry focuses on the basics.

The children's ministry at Hobson runs after school and during the summer. It is called YESSS—an acronym for Youth Empowered for Survival, Service and Self-Esteem.

The survival emphasis includes training in conflict resolution. Says Janet, "Gangs are present in the neighborhood and kids as young as ten may have access to guns or knives. We try to help them figure out alternatives for dealing with anger and conflict so they won't assume violence is the only response. Volunteer counselors—who have learned to be nonviolent when it's really hard—talk with the kids. And the kids listen to them."

The service emphasis is designed to help children be aware of and grateful for their gifts, and to use their gifts for the benefit of the community, Janet says they bake cookies, sing in a nursing home, and help with clean up and recycling projects.

The self-esteem emphasis is based on Psalm 139: "For I am awesomely and wondrously made." Janet says the program's goal is help all the kids in the neighborhood know and believe Psalm 139 to be true about themselves.

Model 86:

Pastor talks with children about sexuality issues.

"We deal a lot around the issue of sexuality, and just valuing yourself," Janet says. "It's common in our neighborhood for girls as young as twelve to be pregnant, and for nobody to be shocked about it. So we have a girls' talk group. Young girls get together and we talk about how you are valued separate and apart from any male. Why is this important? Because lots of young girls—when they are dealing with all the violence and poverty and racism—start thinking the one thing they have that's of value is their body, and they will trade it off to be attached to some older man, thinking he will give them the security and self-esteem they crave."

Model 87:
Church broadens children's views and heightens their dreams.

Hobson's ministry is designed to encourage understanding among people with different backgrounds. In the summer program, kids study a different country each day. Their food, games, and other activities are related to the country they are studying.

"We have several programs where our children hang out with college students," Janet said. "They go on college campuses and join students in everything from basketball games to making posters for special events. Our objective is to help our kids start realizing that they can continue their educations instead of dropping out of high school. We are working toward providing college scholarships for kids who hang in there."

"The church gives kids a place to be and things to do everyday," Janet said. "In our worship service, we don't have a children's time because children's time is all the time. Kids sing, take up the offering, gather prayer cards, make announcements, offer prayers, and read Scripture. We count on them; they know it."

Model 88:
Hobson yokes with other churches.

Hobson has only one full-time staff member in addition to Janet. How does the church maintain such a comprehensive ministry with children? Volunteers carry much of the load.

Hobson "yokes" with other churches. How does yoking work? Larger churches with more people and greater financial resources become partners with smaller churches that have too few people and too little money to minister effectively.

"One of our partners is Brentwood United Methodist," Janet said. "Last summer we had a joint vacation Bible school. Teachers from Hobson teamed up with teachers from Brentwood. It was wonderful for leaders from both churches—as well as for the ninety kids who came."

Hobson also has ongoing partnerships with several other large churches, and works closely with Tying Nashville Together, an advocacy group that has helped secure better wages for nursing home workers, create a neighborhood mediation center, and start seven free, academically oriented, neighborhood-based after-school programs that are funded by the city.

Janet says the children take seriously the three images of the church that the congregation adopted following the intensive Bible study.

"Kids insist that we make the church do what it says it's going to do," she says. "If we say kids are welcomed, then we need to figure out a way to go pick them up. One Sunday I gave a two-minute spiel about evangelism. The next Sunday, the children's population doubled. Those kids just did it. They'd say to me, 'Yeah, I know somebody that needs to come to this church.'"

For a few weeks, Janet picked children up in her seven-passenger van. "Kids would call me all day Saturday. One would say, 'My friend Jimmy wants to come to church. You come by and pick me up and I'll show you where Jimmy lives.' I was spending two hours on Sunday picking up children. Now our church has a fifteen-passenger van and some volunteers to drive, and we pick up a number."

Model 89:
Hobson ministers to residents of homeless shelters.

The church van makes a run on Sunday mornings to homeless shelters in Nashville, and picks up people who want to come to Sunday school and to worship.

People from the shelters were missing a meal by coming to worship because they couldn't make it back from church in time to eat lunch at the shelter. So the church began serving breakfast and lunch every Sunday. Janet says the meals are also welcomed by the children, many of whom come hungry. The church also serves a meal for those who attend Bible study and other activities on Wednesday night.

Model 90:
Hobson helps children feel they are part of the family.

Janet vividly remembers the first children she baptized at Hobson. She shared this story:

"Cynthia (not her real name) was twelve, and she was the classic Pippy Longstocking. Her red-haired sister Leesa (not her real name) was ten. Earlier, their mom had been badly beaten by a guy they were living with. The kids had been abused also, and they were all three running from shelter to shelter. They would always call and tell me where they were, and I would go get them or they would show up. We were planning their baptisms on Easter Sunday. I had sat and talked with their mom and the girls about what baptism is and what a stunning moment it is to become family with all these other folks.

"On Palm Sunday the two girls showed up and said, 'We have to get baptized today because the man found us again last night, and we have to run, and now our grandmother is coming from Florida to pick us up, and we are leaving this afternoon. So that's it.' The girls said their mother was packing and trying to figure out how to be ready to go as soon as they got home from church."

Janet explained to the girls that this was Palm Sunday and the baptism was going to be the next Sunday, on Easter. But Leesa and Cynthia were insistent. "This was it. It was their only chance to be baptized," Janet told me. "It defied our rules and our plans. But we decided to go ahead and baptize those kids, and we did."

As she usually did at the moment of the baptism, Janet invited anyone to come down to the altar and stand with the children. Usually it was the family members who came, but the girls' mom was not there.

A few seconds passed and no one was coming down. Cynthia turned and faced the congregation. With her hands on her hips, she shouted, "Well, I know yawl are coming cause now you are my family."

And Janet says everybody in the church hurried down. "We were all crying over what it meant to baptize these kids who had been through such horrible abuse and who were going to be on the road one more time and probably would never be back with us, but who were still trusting in God's grace that we had loved them and that our love would last, and that God's love was strong enough to last forever.

"It was a holy baptism, a moment when our whole congregation, even people who had not been clearly committed to children's ministry before, began to understand what it might mean and to claim them. They just responded to two kids who loved them."

Janet says within walking distance of Hobson there are many children like Leesa and Cynthia. "They struggle every single day with racism and poverty and violence. And they also struggle with adults who are a source of harm instead of a source of help and hope. It's stunning that these kids deal with so many hard things, and they come to church on their own, laughing and loving, singing and dancing, and dreaming. They are wonderful. Our children have really taught us how to be the church and they are full partners in our congregation."

20.

First United Methodist Church
TULSA, OKLAHOMA

Model 91:
Church adopts elementary school.

"When people are serving out of their passion, the results are phenomenal," says Connie Cole, minister of Community Ministries and Urban Outreach at First Church.

Connie was describing what's happening at Field Elementary School and at Lloyd E. Rader Juvenile Correction Center—two settings where First Church members are reaching out to children and youth.

In 1995, First Church adopted Field Elementary School. With housing projects on three sides, the school has students who are black, Native American, white, Asian, and Hispanic.

The church's ministry to the students includes a store that's stocked with school supplies and clothing that church members provide. Students can make purchases with vouchers—called Big Bucks—that they earn for good behavior, grades, and community involvement. Parents can also earn vouchers by volunteering at the school.

"The store has been so popular and such a good incentive that we have to restock each month," says Connie.

Volunteers from the church—ranging in age from eight to eighty—serve as tutors and mentors to the students.

"It amazes us how many children come to school on a volunteer basis even during the summer months," says Connie.

First Church also serves the students and their families with its other care ministries. Their Eye-Care Ministry provides glasses for one child each month; their Furniture Donations and Needs Ministry gives items to families in the housing project; and their Card Ministry sends cards to the Eugene Field staff.

Students and their parents are also served by First Church's dental, employment, legal counseling, mental health, and used-car ministries.

A new ministry is called "First Friends." Members who participate commit to making one contact each week with their student friend at the school (by letter, phone call, or e-mail) and one personal visit to the school each month.

Students and their families are not the only ones benefiting from First Church's outreach. "Our church members are constantly saying what a blessing the Eugene Field Ministry is to them," says Connie.

Model 92:
Church ministers to children in correctional center.

Inspired by their successful ministry to the school, First Church decided to reach out to more youth with special needs. So a few months ago they began a ministry to Lloyd E. Rader Juvenile Correction Center in Sand Springs, a few miles from Tulsa.

Already thirteen mentor/mentee relationships have been established at the correction center, and nine more will soon begin.

Here's what one mentors says: "My student is really struggling with personal issues. I'm glad I'm here for her each week, and I encourage her as a friend in her time of need and struggle."

Connie says the key to the Eugene Field Elementary School Ministry and the Lloyd E. Rader Juvenile Correction Center Ministry is "getting the right people in the right places at the right time."

She says the church gives extreme care to appropriate screening and training of mentors. "It's been so exciting to see how the Lord has called such inspiring people to make this commitment," Connie said.

21.

God's NET
POMORA, OHIO

Model 93:
Building away from church attracts kids.

Pomora United Methodists have rented a building away from the church, and in it they have developed a ministry called God's NET—Neighborhood Escape For Teens.

The ministry is directed by Keith Raider, who volunteers his time, even though he has little time to spare. Keith is assistant director of a cooperative parish that includes twenty-three United Methodist churches across his county—he pastors three of the churches.

Why do they rent a building when there's plenty of room for God's NET in the church.

Keith explains why: "Our mission is to reach unchurched children and youth. We met at the church for a couple of years, and church kids were the only kids who came. But now that we have a storefront location on the main street we draw a crowd that has had little or nothing to do with churches."

God's NET began four years ago. Since then, 600 children and youth have participated. Last year, 287 took part. Eight out of ten had no church home. Most are from low-income families.

The ministry serves two groups—both work on self-esteem, offer educational enrichment opportunities, are led by people who are good Christian role models, and give the children and youth a safe place to go and fun things to do.

The first group—for ages thirteen through twenty-one—meets every Friday and Saturday night. Music is a big attraction, says Keith, "We play anything from heavy metal to rap, but we only play Christian music. And we stop for prayer and have a devotional each evening. We serve a nourishing meal, thanks to the health department and other agencies that provide the food."

The second group served by God's NET is for children from nine to thirteen. It meets after school on Wednesdays, from three-thirty until five-thirty. Kids play games, listen to music, and receive tutoring. One thing more is included: a thirty-minute Sunday school lesson that's geared for first-time believers.

God's Neighborhood Escape for Teens has its own board of directors, which includes twelve adults, two youth representatives, and the director. More than fifty volunteers help the ministry.

Keith's advice: "Target the audience you want to reach. If you want to reach unchurched children and youth, provide a setting that attracts them, that helps them feel comfortable. Select music they like, put up posters they like, play games they like. But never compromise our Christian faith. Our primary goal is to represent Christ and to help unchurched children and youth experience God's love. If we don't offer kids Christ, we don't have anything to offer them."

He's right. We must not only remember who the people are we are trying to reach; we must also remember who we are and what we are trying to accomplish and why.

22.

Trinity United Methodist Church
LINDSEY, OHIO

Members of Trinity Church made a discovery in the spring of 1997 that startled them.

"We looked around our church and realized that the majority of our children were pretty much grown," says Nancy Ratz, the pastor. "Most of the kids attending our church school were going into the confirmation class. That left three youngsters in the intermediate class, two in primary, and six for the nursery school."

Trinity's children's coordinator, Andrea Smith, spoke up. Standing in the pulpit one Sunday in May, she declared that it was everybody's job to minister to children, and not only to children already in the church. "It's our job to reach children in the community," she declared.

"Some people were troubled, others were bewildered, but everybody prayed, thought, and prayed some more," says Nancy. "We decided we would be like Noah, trusting God and preparing a place for the children, just as Noah built an ark."

"We had done all the right things to encourage community children to come to our church," she continued. "We held a Bible school, we made telephone calls, we sent postcards, we talked to parents, and we had a community picnic. We even talked about changing the time of church school, but nothing seemed to work and our evangelism efforts appeared hopeless.

"So we had another meeting. We talked. We prayed. And then someone said, 'If we can't get the children to come to church school, why don't we take the church school to them?'"

Model 94:
If you can't take kids to church, take the church to kids.

"The discussion ended and everyone went home. We all prayed for guidance, and the idea came! 'Let's make a Jesus Wagon and take it over to the park one evening a week.'"

77

What's a Jesus Wagon?

Nancy explains: "It's a wagon full of things for children to do—games, balls, crayons and coloring books, paper, puzzles, markers, rubber stamps, and books."

During the worship service the next Sunday morning, Nancy announced that the church was going to have a Jesus Wagon for the children.

"Some people were confused about it," she says. Others were skeptical and thought it wouldn't work, and a few had visions of a hayride."

Church member Randy Eppley saw the project's possibilities. "Tell me what you want and I'll build it. I already have the wheels," he said.

Nancy took him up on the offer. She described what a Jesus Wagon should look like, and Randy built it from spare parts.

United Methodist Women and several individuals from the church bought the supplies to stock the wagon—such as children's bulletins, *Pockets* (a United Methodist magazine for kids), and reproducible pages from coloring books and church school materials.

They printed "The Jesus Wagon" on one side in English and on the other side in Spanish so Spanish-speaking children in the community would feel welcomed too.

With their resident clown, "Ladybug," the Jesus Wagon began its weekly trips to the local park.

"During the first week, we had no children," Nancy says. "But two weeks later there were two. And within a few more weeks we had more than a dozen."

Nancy says some of the children now come to church school on Sunday mornings. Others come every Tuesday to the park. "At the beginning of summer, most of the children didn't know why we celebrate Christmas, but they know now."

23.

Saint Mark's United Methodist Church
OKLAHOMA CITY, OKLAHOMA

Model 95:

Young adult class takes vacation Bible school to apartment complex.

During the summer of 1998, a young adult Sunday school class at Saint Mark's reached out to children they had never before reached. How? They took vacation Bible school to an apartment complex.

"The VBS ran for five evenings," says Drew Golding, one of the young adults who participated. "Each evening, we started our session with an outdoor sing-along. The kids were then divided into three different age groups for classes. In class they learned about the Bible through crafts, songs, stories, and games. And, of course, we ended every session with snacks."

Golding says attendance grew from twenty-five on the opening night to thirty-two plus parents on the final night. On Friday night, there was free pizza for all. Vacation Bible school workers from Saint Mark's got a chance to visit with parents and discuss ways to continue the ministry.

A vital key to the success of the VBS, in Drew's judgment, was the cooperation of the apartment's management. "They allowed us to use an empty three-bedroom apartment for air-conditioned classrooms, and they also allowed us to distribute flyers door-to-door advertising the VBS."

Richard Wehrman, minister of missions at Saint Mark's, says the enthusiasm of the children made the event memorable for him. "They met us in the parking lot and helped us unload and set up the tables and chairs each night. Forty-five days have passed since we were there and lots of kids and parents are still talking about how much they enjoyed VBS."

Richard sees the VBS as "a doorway into an otherwise closed community." Through these doors he hopes to build sustained ministries, such as after-school tutoring, Bible studies, and activity times. He expects leadership to emerge from the apartment community to help develop and maintain the ministries.

24.

East Tenth United Methodist Church
INDIANAPOLIS, INDIANA

Good old days at East Tenth Church were a fading memory when the Reverend Darren Cushman-Wood was appointed pastor there in June of 1993.

Founded in 1885, East Tenth had grown steadily until the late 1950s, when its membership topped 2,000 and worship attendance averaged 600. Things were different in 1993. Membership was about 150 and attendance had dropped to fifty. For six months, the church had been without a pastor. Guest preachers filled the pulpit. At least one official of the South Indiana Annual Conference had concluded that East Tenth was dying, and should be closed. And some members agreed.

But East Tenth did not close. It did not die. Today it is very much alive. And it is giving new life to the community, especially to children and youth.

When I visited with Darren in July of 1998, he was beginning his sixth year as pastor of East Tenth, which is his second appointment since completing his seminary work at Union in New York. When I asked what caused East Tenth's decline, Darren said a major factor was demographic changes in the area.

Of course, East Tenth's problems were not limited to changes in the community; factors within the church contributed to the church's decline, Darren points out. Several laypeople who had been the backbone of East Tenth died or moved away. An example: Ray Everson died in 1961. He was editor of an Indianapolis newspaper and taught an adult Sunday school class that averaged 200 in attendance. From 1941 until 1952, the class was broadcast on radio coast to coast.

For a variety of reasons, the congregation began to lose its vision, its sense of mission, and its identity. "That's when the crisis struck," says Darren.

The decline of East Tenth was due to a combination of internal and external factors, and so was its revival. And just as the decline occurred over a period of years, the revival is taking years too.

"When I got here in June of 1993, the first thing we did was go through a long-range planning process," Darren said. "From October of 1993 until June of 1994, our vision team met every week. We used Vision 2000 to help us plan."

Model 96:
Church's "Ezekiel Plan" affirms commitment to kids.

Thinking outside the box, rather than doing business as usual, the vision team came up with what they called "The Ezekiel Plan," named in part for Ezekiel's vision of the valley of the dry bones. At the heart of the plan, was a strong commitment to minister in the community with children and youth.

The first step the vision team took was to look beyond the needs of the church to see the needs of children and youth in the community. The statistical data they gathered reinforced what they had suspected.

"We found that a third of the kids in our neighborhood lived below the poverty level, and half of the adults didn't have a high school education. Our area had the highest teenage pregnancy rate in the state, and our infant mortality rate was twice as high as the national average," Darren recalls.

In addition to gathering statistics, the vision team conducted focus groups with parents, educators, and others involved with children and youth. They did numerous one-on-one visits with children and youth in the neighborhood. What they found indicated that the basic needs and wants were for tutoring with homework, drug education, a safe and pleasant place to hang out, and fun things to do.

"After identifying the needs, we met with various providers of services to children and youth to determine what they were already providing and what more they could provide in cooperation with our church," Darren explains.

Next, the church vision team brainstormed about how God could minister to people in the community—especially children and youth—through East Tenth. What resources did the church have that could be helpful? They listed three major assets, Darren reports.

The first asset was the church property. "We had a building that was in good shape and underutilized. The oldest part—our sanctuary—was built in 1911 and remodeled in the early 1970s. The newest part—the educational wing—was built in 1955."

The second asset was an endowment the church received in the 1960s from Mr. and Mrs. Roy Everson. The original amount had been $300,000, but since most of the interest earnings had been reinvested the endowment had nearly doubled by 1993. The endowment could provide substantial funds for children and youth ministry.

The third asset was tradition. "We had a legacy of over fifteen years of ministering in at least a small way with kids in the neighborhood, and we were committed to doing more," Darren says. Most of the neighborhood ministry had been led by East Tenth's education committee, comprised primarily of women in their sixties, seventies, and eighties.

"Our older women are the real heroes of East Tenth's ministry," says Darren. "They are great examples of the United Methodist Women's tradition of servanthood. Their concern for ministry with children helped us recover our vision, our sense of mission, and our identity. With that recovery, we took on new life."

Darren says Isabelle Mac Kinnon, a key member of the education committee who is now past eighty, came up with the proposal that the church's education wing be turned into a children and youth center.

In the fall of 1994, the administrative council voted to study the proposal. The January 1995 administrative council meeting approved the plan and named a core group to work out the details.

"At a daylong retreat, we put the finishing touches to our mission statement, and did long-range planning," says Darren. "In April 1995, we hired Jean Casmir to direct our center, and by the following December we were incorporated, had received our nonprofit status, and had elected our board of directors."

Here's the relationship the church has with the center: The church's administrative council approves who is elected to the board of directors. The majority of the board members belong to the church and at least 30 percent of the board members are from the community. The church provides the educational wing to the center without charge for rent or utilities. In addition, the church provides some financial assistance to the center to cover expenses. In 1998, the church gave about $15,000 from its endowment.

Darren says the mission of the Children and Youth Center is "to provide a safe place where the spiritual, emotional, educational, and physical needs of children, youth, and their families are responded to in a holistic approach."

To fulfill this mission, the center ministers through an after-school program, a youth drop-in, Little Dove Cooperative Daycare Ministry, and Summer Days for Youth. Since drugs, especially crack, are a critical problem in the community, all ministries of the center have a drug prevention and education component.

Model 97:
After-school program targets children's needs.

Focusing on needs that were confirmed by the research study, the after-school program provides tutoring, homework sessions, recreation, intergenerational, and service opportunities. Designed for age three and up, it meets Monday through Thursday afternoons from four o'clock until six o'clock and on Friday afternoons from four o'clock until five-thirty.

"Kids come right after school and bring their homework," says Casmir, who continues to direct the ministry. "Tutors are there to help them. Most are from East Tenth, some are from a sorority at Butler University."

Model 98:
Youth Drop-In provides positive atmosphere.

The youth drop-in—for boys and girls thirteen through nineteen—is open Saturday and Sunday evenings from six until nine. "There's not a lot in this neighborhood for kids to do," explains Casmir. "Our center gives them a safe place to hang out with friends. They can play basketball or air hockey, shoot pool, read, or just watch television and videos. We have a Bible study on Sundays."

There's no charge for the after-school program or for the youth drop-in. Both ministries are supervised by two paid staff members along with volunteers. Most of the expenses are covered by grants and contributions.

Model 99:
Cooperative daycare helps low-income parents.

Little Dove Cooperative Daycare Ministry started as a service for welfare-to-work parents, many of whom were receiving job training at the Career Corner located across the street from the church. Unlike most daycare centers in the area, Little Dove accepts vouchers from the state.

"Our original intent was to be a cooperative day care center, where the parents participate and have some ownership," Darren said. "We are still evolving this."

Model 100:
Youth Program provides holistic ministry.

Summer Days for Youth is a free program for neighborhood kids ages six to fifteen. On Mondays through Fridays for nine weeks, kids arrive at nine a.m. and stay until four p.m.

"During the mornings, we do educational skill development, drug education, computer art, dance, vocational training, and job-career exploration," says Casmir. "We have a good lunch, and then spend most afternoons swimming, bowling, or enjoying some other recreational activity. We usually have sixty kids in the program and forty on the waiting list."

This program is offered by the church in cooperation with the John H. Boner Community Center, which is located across the street from the church, and the local public school. Darren says East Tenth makes every effort to partner with other agencies so more services can be offered to the children and youth.

Vacation Bible school—offered during the summer—serves eighty kids from the neighborhood. Most leaders are from the church.

Model 101:
Neighborhood kids help the community.

Kids are not only getting a lot from the center," says Casmir. "They are giving a lot back to the community. They help with gardening projects, clean-up projects, and beautification projects throughout the neighborhood."

Darren told me that focusing on the needs and concerns of children and youth in the community has helped the congregation regain what it lost during the decades of decline: its vision, its sense of mission, and its identity.

"We had to redefine ourselves as a congregation," he said. "For many years, we waffled back and forth about whether we were going to be a church with a mission. Now mission is the center piece of who we are. If you join East Tenth, it's because you want to be part of a church that is in mission."

Model 102:
Soup kitchen serves kids and parents.

"We started a soup kitchen in 1997," Darren said. "We call it God's Souper Bowl. About 125 people—including a number of children and youth—come every Sunday evening. We are trying to use this meal also as the context for social services. We have an attorney who comes in once a month to do free legal aid."

Model 103:
Church is advocate for community children.

Now a United Methodist Shalom Zone, East Tenth does community organizing."We have done lobbying to get more funding for health care in the community, and we've organized drug prevention marches. We also set up a small loan fund to help people buy cars so they can go back to work."

The new-found sense of mission is building morale and commitment.

"Up to this point, our emphasis has been on regaining our vision, sense of mission, and identity. Those things had to come first," he said. "We have changed our worship around so it is more inviting. Now our evangelism committee is getting more intentional about reaching out to the community. We are doing home visits, house blessings, those sorts of things to let our neighbors know East Tenth is their church."

I asked Darren what had been the most satisfying reward he has received as pastor of Tenth Street.

"Being able to work with this congregation," he said. "I appreciate their willingness to try new things, their openness to change. They've also challenged me to put away some of my prejudices about older adults. Their witness of servanthood has been the biggest blessing I have received. They are a good example of one generation blessing the next generation."

25.

Grace United Church
KANSAS CITY, MISSOURI

"When I was growing up on a farm in Southwest Missouri, I thought I'd live forever," said the Reverend Sharon Garfield, "but kids around our church wonder if they'll live to be twenty-one. And I understand why they wonder."

I was visiting with Sharon in the study at Grace Church, where she has been pastor since 1990. She was telling me how her church ministers to children and youth in her neighborhood.

"This is one of the most racially and ethnically diverse parts of Kansas City," Sharon explained. "Just a few blocks west of us is where hundreds of refugees from Haiti, Sudan, and the former Soviet Union settle every year, but most of the people right around our church are African American, Native Americans, or Latinos. We have a few Anglos."

Despite their racial differences, she says, all the residents have at least one thing in common: they are poor. "They have settled here because housing is available and affordable, even though its neither adequate nor appealing."

When Sharon and I drove through the area around Ninth Street and Benton Boulevard, where Grace is located, we saw many two-story and three-story-houses—some have what used to be servant's quarters. Before white flight and other changes in the 1960s, they were the homes of upper-income families.

"Most of these houses have been divided in to apartments and have several families living in them," Sharon said. "Lots of the people are unemployed. Nearly everyone who has a job works for minimum wage. They move out of here as soon as they can."

What is life like for children and youth who live in the area? "Most are unsupervised," Sharon said. "A lot of parents don't make enough on their jobs to have a baby sitter, so there's no adult present when the kids come home from school. Some parents who are at home are dysfunctional because they drink heavily, use drugs or have other problems. Their kids are pretty much on their own, with very little to do."

Sharon's desire to help kids cope with poverty, drugs, violence and other perils motivated her to ask the Missouri West Conference of The United Methodist Church to appoint her as pastor of Grace United, which is a combined congregation of the former Grace Presbyterian and Independence Avenue United Methodist churches.

During the early 1960s, Grace had 800 members and Independence Avenue had 2,400. When Sharon became pastor of Grace United in 1990, attendance at worship was eighteen—all the members were white and all were over sixty. Now—in January 1998—the average worship attendance has climbed to 150. The congregation includes a balanced mix of residents in the area: black, Latino, and white. To serve the growing number of Latinos, the eleven thirty Sunday worship service is in Spanish, led by Grace's associate pastor, who is Hispanic. The worship celebration in English starts at ten o'clock, and a bilingual church school starts at nine o'clock.

In addition to its Sunday services, Grace United serves more than 2,500 persons each month with a variety of ministries. They have one of the largest food pantries in Kansas City, a Cocaine Anonymous group, a job readiness component for teens, and an after-school program for younger children. Grace United also works closely with a battered women's shelter, which Sharon founded and directed during the 1980s.

Model 104:
PeaceMaking Academy teaches kids to live in peace.

Grace United PeaceMaking Academy—an eight-week summer program for neighborhood children from age three to fourteen— was developed by Sharon soon after she became pastor at Grace. Attendance at the 1997 PeaceMaking Academy was 232. Here's Sharon's description of why and how the academy got started:

"Reaching into the community and listening to people and getting to know them made me painfully aware that many children are caught up in violent situations. Even in those cases where violence isn't going on in the home, kids are exposed to it just living in a community like this where poverty is the rule and racial tension is so high.

As she reflected on the domestic violence that was occurring in the area, she remembered what she had learned a decade earlier when she was the founding director of the first shelter for battered women in Kansas City. "I had seen that violence has a cycle of its own, and that if you don't break that cycle, the one who may be the victim as a small child is likely to become the abuser as an adult. So my goal was for our church to come up with a way to break the cycle.

Model 105:

Vacation Bible school launches neighborhood ministry.

"I decided the best place to start was with the children of the neighborhood, because I felt that their needs were the greatest," Sharon recalls. "So one afternoon I went visiting in the streets around the church, inviting children to a vacation Bible school, and within thirty minutes I had over seventy children who wanted to come.

"We met every morning, using our United Methodist vacation Bible school curriculum and doing the traditional things that most churches do," Sharon says. "At the end of the week, kids were asking, 'Why can't this go on?' So I was convinced that we needed to do more."

After determining what the kids seemed to need most, she designed a curriculum to address those needs. And the PeaceMaking Academy was born.

Model 106:

Grace builds ministry on Bible study.

"I believe people need to have a strong foundation to build their lives on and guide them to wise decisions. And I believe the Bible and the Christian values are the place to start. So when I began working on a curriculum for the PeaceMaking Academy, I turned to the Christian Scriptures. The Bible became our basic text.

"I develop a daily Bible study that focused on a different theme of peacemaking for each of the eight weeks of the Academy. I pulled out Scriptures for the first week that would help the children see Jesus as a peacemaker. The next week we examined how Jesus dealt with violence personally. Then the next week we identified the principles Jesus taught for getting along peacefully with others. Another week we looked at what Jesus promised about finding peace within your self, even when you are in the midst of conflict and violence. Each week the children learned a memory verse that summed up the theme for that week."

Numerous changes have been made in the PeaceMaking Academy since it began, but Bible study is still the heart of curriculum. Other components include conflict resolution, anger control, and cultural awareness.

Model 107:

Former gang member teaches conflict resolution.

"Around here, when somebody gets in your face, your first tendency is to smack him in the face," Sharon said. "When children see adults—including their parents—settle conflicts with their fists, it's really hard to get them to begin thinking in other ways. That's why we include conflict resolution as a major component of our academy.

"For the first couple of years, we brought in professionals to teach conflict resolution. They did a good job, but in 1996 we did something different and it worked even better. Angel Gussman, a teenager who had been a student at our Academy our first summer, was working with us as an assistant. When he found out that the professional who had been teaching the conflict management group wasn't coming, he asked us to let him teach it.

"We knew Angel was a former gang member and that he had done a lot of conflict resolution study as part of getting his own act together. So we decided to let him teach the class. And he did a wonderful job. When he talked, he spoke the kids' language, and they really listened. He taught the class again in the summer of 1997 and has became one of our best teachers. Now he's eighteen and his career goal is to work with children."

Model 108:
Anger control group helps kids control themselves.

The academy's anger control group helps children develop healthy ways to cope with prejudice, peer pressure, dominating authority figures, hostility, and other provocation.

"We want the kids to learn that there are ways to control their tempers, and there are ways you can become a winner and the other person can become a winner and nobody will be a loser. They need to learn this because the stakes are high especially for young people in this community. Death is right around the corner. Many of these kids truly don't believe they will live to be more than twenty or twenty-five. But if they learn to control their anger, they will have a much better chance of surviving.

Sharon says one day when she visited the anger control group they were discussing what happens when you are at school and one of your peers starts threatening you.

"An eight-year-old girl told about an older boy trying to get her involved in one of the gangs. She felt very pressured, was afraid, and didn't know how to handle it. The adult leading our group asked the kids what they had done—or what they would do—in similar situations. They shared ideas for ten minutes or so. Then the leader asked the kids to examine each option that had been suggested, to think through the possible consequence of each, and to discuss what would be the best response. After the session was over, the girl said it really helped her to express her anger to the group, to learn that she wasn't the only one who had encountered the problem, and to hear suggestions for how she could control her temper next time she encountered a similar situation."

Model 109:
Church helps kids respect other cultures.

One critical need in the area around Grace United, Sharon points out, is for people of diverse racial and ethnic groups to develop greater appreciation for their own cultures and for the cultures of others.

During the eight weeks that the academy meets, two weeks are devoted to the four major cultures represented in the community: African American, Latino, Native American, and Anglo American.

"When we are focusing on the African American culture," Sharon explains, "all of our field trips are to African American points of interest. We do African dances, we teach the kids how to play African drums. Our art projects and even the games we play are from Africa.

"So before their two weeks are over, our African American children begin to find out more their about own heritage and they develop more pride in their culture. This helps their self-esteem. Meanwhile, the children who are not African Americans begin to see the unique gifts that their African American brothers and sisters bring to the community. We follow the same plan with the other three cultures."

Sharon says as the kids become more aware of their cultures and the cultures of their neighbors they become more understanding and get along with fewer conflicts.

"The problem is eight weeks in the summer is way to short a time to accomplish all that needs to be done," she acknowledged. "What we plan to do this coming summer is to concentrate on just the African American and Latinos since they make up the majority of the academy. And we are also doing more cultural awareness study throughout the year in our other programs."

One way that the PeaceMaking Academy helps children and youth get along with one another is by helping them learn to communicate, says Shirley Paschal who directs the academy.

She says fights often break out because somebody thinks someone is putting him or her down. Many times the guilty party doesn't realize what he or she said or did that upset the other person.

"A while back some of our teenagers were to the point they were polarized between the Latinos and the African American and Anglo American kids," Shirley said. "When we tried to talk to them about it, the whole thing was: 'They don't have any respect for me.'

"We got them to sit down together and start talking. They were using as an example riding the bus. African Americans and Anglo Americans were saying, 'Well, I get on the bus and the Latinos don't say hello or whatever.' " After they talked for a few minutes in the group, they found that fear and the language barrier was a big part of their problem.

"A lot of the Latino children don't speak English very well, you can barely understand what they are saying, and others are very reserved. They are inclined to stick together. The black and white children thought the Latinos were stuck up and stand offish, and concluded they didn't respect them or like them. They started getting along better after they got to know one another and overcame their fear and misconceptions."

Model 110:
Good evaluation leads to better ministry.

Following each academy, Sharon and her coworkers, along with the children and youth, have evaluated what has happened during the eight weeks. Building on strengths and learning from experience, they have made adjustments for the next summer.

"We haven't found any magic answers," Sharon admits. "But we are finding ways to improve." She cites as an example a change they have made in teacher assignments.

"We started out assigning our instructors to a group of children that they would be with all day," Sharon says. "This system kept our cost down, but it created problems. The teacher was responsible for the Bible study, arts and crafts, and music. The problem was our teachers were not gifted in all areas.

"In 1997, we decided to use a model that's similar to a school system. We hired persons with skills in a particular area, and they taught that area to everyone—the classes rotated. This system has its problems, too. It means that if you are teaching conflict resolution, you have to figure out how to present that material to a three-year-old one hour and to a thirteen-year-old the next. Obviously that's a challenge. But this is working best for us."

When I asked Sharon what impact the PeaceMaking Academy is having on the children, she told me about LaBrenda, who was a first-grader when she first came to the PeaceMaking Academy during the summer of 1992.

"At first, LaBrenda didn't have anything to do with the other kids," Sharon said. "She just sat in a corner by herself, in a fetal position, with her thumb in her mouth, afraid of everyone."

Sharon says she understood why the seven-year-old child was frightened. Six members of her extended family had been killed within two years, either in drive-by shootings, gang fights, or domestic abuse. One victim was her fourteen-year-old cousin, who was the mother of a year-old child. She had tried to protect her mother, who was being beaten up by her mother's boyfriend. When she intervened, her mother's boyfriend shot her to death.

One of the most encouraging results of that summer's academy was the progress LaBrenda made, Sharon said. "After three or four weeks, she started coming out of her protective shell. And by the eighth week she was giggling and talking all the time. We were thrilled!"

Sharon said another child who came to the Academy would throw tantrums and physically hurt herself, but wouldn't hurt anyone else. "She would smash her head into the wall, bite and scratch herself, almost become catatonic. She did this for four weeks, but after that she relaxed and calmed down. By the end of the academy she was mixing in with the other children and having lots of fun."

Sharon says she and her staff see plenty of evidence that the academy is making a difference for the children and youth it serves.

"We haven't done as much tracking and evaluation as we should," she says. "Up to now we just haven't had the time or the resources. But we are beginning to get some really important data. Of the 236 children who attended our academy in 1997, we don't have much information on fifty-four. Of the remaining 182, we know that at least 119 were living in violent situations, more than 100 were living in homes where alcohol and drugs were heavily used by either one of both parents. We had nine children that we know had been sexually molested, and we suspect there were many more."

Sharon declares that she and her staff don't profess to have all the answers to questions facing children and youth in poverty stricken areas, but she believes the basic principles and procedures of the PeaceMaking Academy are producing positive results.

"We know the academy has turned our church around and moved it from dying to being a growing church. And we believe it is also giving new life to the children and youth and to this whole community. We offer a safe environment that helps children discover they are not trapped. They learn that they do have choices in how they get along with others and in what they do with their lives. They begin to realize that they are not doomed to an early death."

26.

Theressa Hoover United Methodist Church
LITTLE ROCK, ARKANSAS

Theressa Hoover Church helps children by helping their parents recover from alcohol and drug dependency.

Model 111:
Church provides residential drug treatment.

The church is certified by the state of Arkansas as a treatment provider for chemically dependent persons. Don Wilson, associate pastor at Theressa Hoover, says the program focuses on helping persons who have been dual diagnosed—who have some other problem in addition to chemical dependency that prevents them from caring for themselves.

The church has bought several nearby houses to use in its residential care program. Says Wilson: "The houses provide a chemically free transitional living environment for the people while they are getting on their feet."

Participants in the rehabilitation program receive vocational counseling and job training. The church also helps them find jobs. Some people complete the program in six months, and some require as long as eighteen months, Wilson observed. After they are employed and living on their own, they start paying the church a modest fee for the services they have received.

Theressa Hoover also serves kids in other ways, including a summertime program and an after-school program, both of which are designed to help kids who are at risk.

The Reverend William Robinson, Jr., has been senior pastor of Theressa Hoover since 1970, and has led in the development of numerous ministries for people in the low-income neighborhood.

27.

Oakdale United Methodist Church
GRAND RAPIDS, MICHIGAN

Model 112:
Church hosts neighborhood minifair.

Every summer since 1984, Oakdale Church has invited people from the neighborhood to a minifair. Usually about 150 people—mostly children—gather at the church for games and other fun activities.

"The fair helps our neighbors know our church is here for them," says the Reverend Marguerite Rivera-Bermann, pastor of the 100-member congregation. That's not all. She believes it provides a place for the diverse population of the highly mobile area to get acquainted with one another. And she believes the good feelings the fair builds have helped the church develop two new ministries: Thrilling Thursdays and K-O.

Model 113:
After-school program includes Bible study.

Thrilling Thursdays—an activity on, you guessed it, Thursdays—gives neighborhood kids a safe and enriching place to come after school. Not only do they play games and eat snacks, they also receive fifteen minutes of biblically based religious education. For many, that's fifteen minutes more than they receive anywhere else, Marguerite observes.

Model 114:
Church forms gang.

KO is an alternative gang that Oakdale organized and operates in collaboration with three other United Methodist churches. Youth participating in the program are recruited from existing gangs in the Grand Rapids area.

Referrals come primarily from the local elementary schools and the juvenile court system.

According to Marguerite, KO is designed to encourage positive development of youth. It encourages dialogue and debate on issues related to youth and utilizes preventative activities to enhance leadership skills and spiritual questing.

What does KO stand for? Several things, Marguerite explains. Including "Keep On Keeping On," "Kick Open Closed Doors," and "Kick Out Bad Thoughts."

KO is still under development, Marguerite explains. "We are striving for an ongoing five-day-a-week program that provides a safe place for kids to come immediately following school to do homework, make friends, play games, and eat snacks. It's a therapeutic model—everyone has a chance to share his or her joys and concerns. We have a spiritual developmental time to help kids realize that within themselves there is a firm ground for faith."

Codirecting KO with Marguerite is Jose Jimenez, a therapeutic counselor with gang experience. Under Jose's leadership, Young Lords—a major gang in Chicago during the 1960s and 1970s—began social outreach ministries in a United Methodist church.

Shared Mission Focus on Young People—an initiative of The United Methodist Church—awarded Oakdale a pilot grant to help them develop KO.

For more information about Oakdale's ministry for children and youth, write the Reverend Marguerite Rivera-Bermann, 324 Griswold SE, Grand Rapids, MI 49507.

28.

East Nashville Neighborhood Outreach Ministry
NASHVILLE, TENNESSEE

Many churches across the nation are finding that one of the most effective ways they can reach children in the community is by providing a mentoring ministry.

How can a church build a mentoring ministry that really helps children get off to a good start in school and in life?

I asked an expert. Roxie Williams has been building effective mentoring ministries since 1982. A Board of Global Ministries church and community worker, Roxie is director of East Nashville Neighborhood Outreach Ministry (ENOM). She works with nine United Methodist churches in East Nashville, assisting them with mentoring and other ministries.

Model 115:
Mentors must be good role models.

"For mentoring to really help children," she says, "you must have volunteers who love kids, who are good role models for them, and who take this ministry seriously."

Where does she find them? Many are members of the nine churches she works with, but some come from outside the low income neighborhood. She visits churches across Nashville, talking to groups about how mentors help children, appealing to people of all ages who want to be part of a hands-on ministry that touches lives.

As a result of her appeals, several prospering United Methodist churches are yoking with the inner-city churches, providing volunteers and financial assistance for this ministry. Volunteers are also coming from Vanderbilt University and other colleges in the area.

"Many of our best prospects are older people who have retired and can spend an hour or two working with children. Some shy away from tutoring, which they think of as teaching. They say, 'I went to school fifty years ago. I don't know how to teach the new methods.' But they are inclined to help when we invite them to be mentors. We explain that being a mentor is primarily just being a friend to the child, and we assure them that we will give them the training they need to do what we expect of them."

Model 116:
Give volunteers job descriptions.

It is vitally important for volunteers to know precisely what is expected of them, Roxie points out. "We give our mentors a job description. It emphasizes how mentoring is an important ministry, how we expect them to take it seriously, to be there every day, and to let us know when they are not going to be there. It elevates them to unpaid staff status and gives them accountability and freedom."

Model 117:
Orientation and training prepares volunteers.

Mentors receive initial training at an orientation session. "At the orientation, we assure our mentors that we want them to help children learn academics so they can make steady progress in school, and we promise the mentors that we will help them develop the skills they need for that important task. But we remind them that the most important thing they can do is model God's love through a caring relationship. If a child can have one adult for ninety minutes once a week who really listens to him, who really wants to know what's going on in his life, it's going to help him feel special and loved and hopeful. That's what we are all about."

Once the mentors have agreed to work, have been given a job description, and have gone through orientation, what happens then? Are they left to sink or swim? By no means. Roxie follows through on the promise to help them develop the skills and to acquire the knowledge they need for their tasks.

Model 118:
Enrichment workshops strengthen the spirit and skills.

Every other month there's an enrichment workshop for the volunteers. By working closely with the mentors, Roxie finds out what they know, what they need to know, and what they want to know. The enrichment workshops address those needs and concerns. She often brings in experts to lecture and answer questions.

At one workshop a psychology professor from Vanderbilt University talked about hyperactivity and offered suggestions to help mentors relate to children with attention deficit disorder.

"A teacher at University School comes every year to talk about how to get along with the children, what to expect from them, and what to expect from your session with them," says Roxie. "She always has some marvelous handouts that help our mentors form some realistic expectations, so they are not expecting results that are not going to come."

Often visible results are slow in coming, and sometimes mentors feel that they are accomplishing nothing, as illustrated by this story Roxie shared with me:

"Harvel, who was about seventy-three, had been working for nearly six weeks with a kindergarten child. The child lived across the street from me, and I saw him play all the time and I knew he could talk. But he didn't talk in school.

"I assigned him to Harvel, because they were both such gentle souls. They took off down to their little room to study. After the session, Harvel came into the kitchen where I was and he said, 'I can't teach that youngster. I'm not teaching him anything.'

"I said, 'Harvel, you don't have to teach him anything. That child went out of here with a smile on his face, and that was worth whatever time you spent with him. If he shows up next week, you just be with him.'

"For several months, Harvel finished every session saying, `I didn't teach him anything.' But finally that little child started talking, not just with us at the church, but also at the school. He came out of his shell that year because of Harvel."

Roxie is always there to affirm the mentors and be supportive of them.

"You work closely with the volunteers," she said. "You train them, you help them feel that you don't expect overnight results, you stay in there with them even when there are no signs of progress. You remind them to just plant seeds and to trust in God for the harvest."

29.

First United Methodist Church
LITTLE ROCK, ARKANSAS

The assassination of Dr. Martin Luther King Jr. in April 1968, caused the Koinonia Sunday school class at First Church to do a lot of soul searching. As a practical response to King's death, the class of young couples and young singles wanted to reach out to the black community in a tangible way that would significantly help.

To determine needs of the black community and to explore how the class could help, they asked several black leaders to join them on Sunday morning and in special evening sessions. One of the black leaders, Sonny Walker, head of the Little Rock office of the Economic Opportunity Agency, pinpointed a problem that challenged the class to take action.

Waller told them that even though black persons could no longer be barred from equal employment opportunity, many black women could not take advantage of this opportunity because there was not affordable and reliable day care for them and so they were forced to stay home to care for their children. He said that if a way could be found to give young black mothers the freedom to seek better paying jobs, this could ultimately increases the income, the standard of living, and the economic opportunities of all blacks—one of Dr. King's objectives.

As class members reflected on this need, they observed that their church had a well-equipped preschool facility that was unused six days a week. The concept of a subsidized day-care program, open to all but nevertheless deliberately reaching out to black members, took root. The class wanted the facility to be integrated so it would bring more social contact between the races. And, preliminary studies indicated sliding-scale fees could be charged that seemed within the ability of parents it would serve, provided the center received a subsidy that was within the resources of First Church.

Major hurdles surfaced, but one by one they were overcome, thanks to generous support from congregational leaders and the senior pastor. The church board gave full approval to the proposal to open the day care center and to subsidize approximately half of its operating budget, in addition to furnishing utilities, maintenance, and custodial care at no charge.

Model 119:
Daycare center serves parents who work downtown.

The day care center opened in September 1969 with an enrollment of about sixty children and a staff dedicated to the mission of the center. Fees were based on family income and needs, with a few full scholarship available. For some children, it was their first social exposure outside the home. Many were painfully withdrawn and shy. For some, their previous "day-care" had been furnished by an older brother or sister, sometimes only of elementary school age themselves. The staff observed many touching instances of lives enriched by participation in the day care center, and they shared these moving reports with the church board and the congregation.

But within a year after the day care center opened, the federal government began to address the problem that First Church was addressing. Federally funded facilities were opened that offered day care for preschoolers at even more affordable fees. The church's center eventually lost many of its children to these new facilities and was faced with the options of simply closing or of refocusing its mission.

First Church and the day care center board decided to move toward an integrated mix of families who could afford slightly higher rates for a superior level of services, still supported by a subsidy from the church.

In 1985, the church bought a building across from the church. At first they considered using the property to expand parking, but they decided instead that there was a greater need for expanding the child care facilities.

As a result of that decision, the Gertrude Remmel Butler Child Development Center at First Church now has its own specially designed and equipped $1.5 million facility, which has three fire-rated stairways with outside exits, a sprinkler system throughout the building, monitoring cameras for all exits, and an intercom to all rooms.

On the second floor of the center, there's an in-door fresh air playground that covers 7,500 square feet and is equipped with all the features of an outdoor playground where children can run and play regardless of weather.

Staff qualifications include a nurturing, caring nature, with a true concern for young children and their families. In-house workshops by pediatricians and psychologists provide the staff with the latest techniques in developmentally appropriate early childhood training.

"Our Christian environment helps each child become aware that every person is worthy of God's love and the love of others," says Jenny Adair, director of the center. "Our program, staff, and facilities provide a loving atmosphere that nurtures physical, social, mental, emotional, and spiritual growth."

When I toured the center in the spring of 1998, the enrollment of preschool children was 210, and the center had sixty-six people on its payroll. An additional 110 school children were expected to come during the school vacation months. The center continues to be a nonprofit ministry of First Church.

According to the Children's Defense Fund, in 1997 three out of five American preschoolers were in child care, and nearly five million children were home alone after school each week.

"Children's experiences in child care and after-school programs help shape the way they think, learn, and behave for the rest of their lives," a CDF publication points out. "Yet much of the care we offer children is woefully inadequate. Six out of seven child care centers offer mediocre to poor care, according to a recent national study by a group of universities. Half of the rooms in child care centers were judged to be potentially harmful to infants and toddlers. And forty-one states require no training for providers before they can offer child care serves in their homes."

First Church is one of many United Methodist churches across the nation that are committed to providing child care and after-school programs. By following the model establishing by John Wesley when he reached out to children in England two centuries ago, they are setting the standards for child care excellence in their areas.

30.

Other Models That Reach Children

Here are some other creative models churches use to reach children and their families:

Model 120:
Breakfast for school children attracts kids.

When Emile Tosso became pastor of the United Methodist Church in Loranger, Louisiana, he recognized that his church had an excellent location for ministering to children and youth: the elementary, junior high, and high schools surrounded the church.

Under conviction to minister to the kids, Emile explored ways to reach them and develop healthful relationships. And he had an idea: invite the kids over for a free breakfast followed by a ten-minute devotional.

The kids responded. Some mornings seventy kids come. At first, Emile was doing the breakfast himself, but when people in his church saw what an impact it was having on the children and youth they started helping prepare and serve the food. Word got around the community, and the church began receiving checks from folks who wanted to help the ministry grow.

Emile tells me the kids are coming for more than fellowship and pancakes. They are also hungry for spiritual nurture.

Model 121:
Church invites public to free parenting classes.

First United Methodist Church in Henryetta, Oklahoma has well-qualified leaders for this community service. Classes last for six weeks. Child care is provided.

Model 122:
Church collects clothes and food for needy.

Members of Grand Avenue United Methodist Church in McAlester, Oklahoma, collect infant clothes and take them to the local hospital for new mothers who have no clothing for their newborn babies. During the Christmas season, each Sunday school class collects food for families of persons in the state prison, which is located in McAlester, and for others in the community with special needs. They host a Christmas party for low-income families in the fellowship hall with games, refreshments, and gifts.

Model 123:
Church helps children get ready for school.

In July 1998, First United Methodist Church in Claremore, Oklahoma established a task force to study children and poverty in the area. In August, a panel of professionals involved in social services made a presentation to adult Sunday school classes to heighten awarness of the plight of children in an impoverished area.

In response to what they had learned from their task force and the panel, the United Methodists launched an effort to raise funds to help kids with school supplies.

Church members contributed to the cause and also invited others in the community to help. They raised $4,300, and a store contributed an additional $3,000. By the end of the first week of school, the church presented backpacks and other school supplies to 356 children.

Part Four

Ministry to Children in Economic Poverty

31.

Ministry with the Poor and Marginalized
TENNESSEE ANNUAL CONFERENCE

In 1996, the Tennessee Conference of The United Methodist Church chose as its top priority ministry with the poor and marginalized. Every church in the conference was to designate a person to coordinate local efforts to implement the priority.

Model 124:
Churches organize for ministry with poor.

If your church would like to create a similar position, perhaps you will find the job description the Tennessee Conference developed helpful. It declares that the local church coordinator of Ministry with the Poor and Marginalized is not to take on the congregation's mission, charity, and outreach work alone.

"The coordinator's job is also not necessarily to start a new church program or project to help poor people. It is not necessarily to do more, to work harder, or to set up yet another bureaucracy. It is not to save the world, or to make poor people think, talk, look and act like middle-class people. It probably has more do with allowing God to change us than it does with changing them. And it is not to save their souls, although it may well have something to do with saving our souls. Further, it is not just a matter of 'benevolences,' missions, or Christian social concerns. Finally, it is not about the congregation as a whole being either Democrat or Republican, or liberal or conservative. It is a matter of being serious Christian disciples."

According to the Tennessee Conference job description, the task of a local church coordinator has four components: "to motivate, to educate, to organize, and to evaluate the congregation concerning its faithfulness and effectiveness in ministry with people who have to struggle just to survive."

For more information about this model, contact Harmon Wray, Tennessee Conference Coordinator of Ministry with the Poor and Marginalized, P. O. Box 120607, Nashville, Tenn. 377212. Phone (615) 329-1177.

32.

Bible Study About the Poor
TENNESSEE CONFERENCE

"If we are truly biblical and truly Wesleyan, it will drastically transform who we are as a people, how we think about church, and what we do in church," says Harmon L. Wray, coordinator of Ministries With the Poor and Marginalized for Tennessee Conference.

"We will begin to see who we are and what we do through the eyes of poor people when we get to know them in a long-term relationship, and pretty soon there won't be any them and us. Not only will barriers break down, some strong advocacy will spring up from the church in solidarity with poor folks around economic justice issues."

Model 125:
Bible study prepares for ministry with poor.

Inspired by Harmon's leadership, a Bible study was developed in 1996 by the Tennessee Conference Task Force on Ministries With the Poor and Marginalized. Called "Back to the Bible: God's Call to Partnership with the Poor," the study was distributed to churches across the Tennessee Conference.

In the eight-week study there's a letter from Kenneth Carder, bishop of the Nashville Area, which begins with this statement: "My commitment to ministry with economically impoverished persons is built on two foundations—the Bible's witness to Jesus Christ and my own personal experience growing up in poverty."

Bishop Carder says growing up in a "loving family of sharecroppers" confirmed the Bible's witness to Christ's presence among the poor. "Without the church's witness in word and deed that 'Jesus loves me,' my impoverished world would have defined me. The church accepted me and welcomed my gifts for ministry."

The bishop declares that God is calling The United Methodist Church to recover its biblical and historic roots among the poor, who are both recipients and means of God's grace. And he suggests that a good place to start is with Bible study.

The Tennessee Conference Bible study focuses on seven Scripture passages and one closing study/worship experience. Placed in a three-ring notebook binder, there's a student's guide and a leader's guide for each session. The student's guide includes a brief biblical background, quotes from Bible scholars, and reflections on the passage from impoverished or marginalized persons in Tennessee. Questions for discussion are also included. The leader's guide offers teaching suggestions and possible answers to questions that might be raised.

For more information about the Bible study, you may contact Harmon Wray, P. O. Box 120607, Nashville, Tenn. 377212. Phone (615) 329-1177.

33.

Ministries with the Poor
MISSISSIPPI ANNUAL CONFERENCE

Angie Williams, who directs the Episcopal Initiative on Children and Poverty for Mississippi, has shared with me the following models that illustrate ways churches are responding to the plight of children and their families who are living below the poverty level.

Model 126:
Class helps mother go from welfare to work.

Mississippi's welfare rolls have been cut in half since 1993 and a United Methodist church in the state is doing its part to help one mother on welfare find independence and financial security for herself and her three children.

Wesley Sunday school class at First United Methodist Church in Brandon has led the way for involving the whole church in putting love into action.

"Previously, our class was volunteering at a local service agency, but we felt called to a different kind of ministry, reports class member Claire Nowlin. "We began looking for a more meaningful opportunity to serve, one where we might have a more significant impact.

The class, realizing that the church has an important role to play if welfare reform is to succeed, decided to help a family make the transition off welfare. When they contacted the Economic Assistance Office at the Rankin County Department of Human Services, they were given several vignettes of potential families in their area.

The family they selected was a single mother with three children. Before she would agree to the arrangement, the mother requested a meeting. She was concerned about how invasive the class would be. A meeting was arranged with the DHS social worker, the mother, and a representative from the Sunday school class.

In that initial meeting, the mother shared what she needed: a job, transportation, adequate clothing, and firewood. The Sunday school class sought help from the whole congregation. Someone donated a car. The class raised money to replace tires and hoses, install a new headliner, and paint the vehicle. They also purchased the car tag and agreed to pay the insurance for six months. They purchased school supplies and clothes for the children, provided firewood, and even found the mother a job.

"Our Sunday school class has been working with this family for more than a year now," Claire reported in July 1998. "The mother enjoys her job and is doing well at it. Now she's has taken over her insurance payments. It has been such a positive experience for the class and the church that we are planning to help a second family. This experience has helped us understand the plight and practical problems facing those in poverty. It has reminded us that we are blessed and that blessings come with a certain responsibility to our brothers and sisters in Christ."

Model 127:
Churches help low-income senior adult get better housing.

A small, rural cluster of churches in the Scott-Rankin County area of Mississippi became aware that a senior adult and her twelve-year-old granddaughter were living in a house that had holes in the ceiling and holes in the floor.

"There was no indoor bathroom and no heating," says Reverend Rayford Woodrick of the East Jackson District program staff. "Because of the family's income and other factors, they didn't meet eligibility requirements for other agencies working to provide adequate housing. They simply fell between the cracks in the system."

The need was brought to the attention of a cluster of churches, and the cluster decided to help meet the need. A task group was formed primarily from the cluster churches, and included representatives from Baptist church, a Presbyterian church, and a Missionary Baptist church.

The group found a used mobile home priced at $6,000. The district staff helped arrange an appraisal, and when it was found to be a good buy, they recommended that the mobile home be purchased and relocated for the family. A member of the task group arranged a loan until the $6,000 could be raised, which didn't take long. Work teams prepared the mobile home and the new site for the move. In early 1998, the mobile home was moved, set up with running water, gas, and a septic tank.

"When the grandmother and her granddaughter moved into their new home, a local reporter did a story on what had happened," says Rayford. "The grandmother told the reporter that no one had ever cared for her like the Methodists had before, that no one had ever gone out of their way to do something good for her. The television story stimulated additional responses from the larger community."

Providing housing for one family is a small but significant step, Rayford observes. "It was significant for that family, and it was significant for the churches involved. Those churches and the community now have a better understanding of ministry. They have grown closer to God and closer to one another across congregational, community, and racial lines."

Model 128:
Church sponsors day camp for low-income children.

Mount Zion United Methodist Church at DeLisle is a seventy-six-member African-American church located in Pass Christian, Mississippi. Mount Zion is growing. From June 1996 until June 1998, their membership more than doubled, and for two years the church has been the driving force behind a summer day camp that serves from 130 to 150 children.

When Reverend Rosemary Williams came to Mount Zion four years ago, she shared with her new congregation her past experiences with a summer day camp for children. Reverend Williams envisioned the same kind of day camp for the children in the community around Mount Zion. But the congregation was cautious. Could the church afford to sponsor such a camp?

Today Camp Seashore, sponsored by Mount Zion, has a budget of $30,000 and serves all children from the community, which includes black, white, and Asian American.

The camp is open five days a week for six weeks during the summer. The day begins at 7:45 a.m. and ends at 5:30 p.m. Parents pay $25 a week for a child to attend. Discounts and scholarships are available for families who need them.

"Camp Seashore wouldn't be possible without the help and support of the entire congregation and community," says Rosemary. "Twenty full-time volunteers manage the day-to-day activities. Meals for the children are provided through the United States Department of Agriculture feeding program. The Harrison County Board of Supervisors and DuPont provide transportation to and from various field trips. The local elementary school and headstart center donate space for the camp on alternate years."

Children at Camp Seashore enjoy arts and crafts, music, sports, a reading program, a talent show, and much more. One or two days a week there are field trips for skating, bowling, swimming, and tours of museums and farms. Through Camp Seashore, Mount Zion offers children and families of the community a safe alternative to summer care.

Model 129:
Church brightens Christmas for needy families.

In 1960, Wesley United Methodist Church in Jackson, Mississippi saw a need and found the resources to "adopt" a small number of families to offer them Christmas gifts and ample food for the holidays, things these families probably would not have enjoyed otherwise. Called "Birthday Gifts for Christ," the Christmas mission program continues to brighten lives even though the Wesley congregation no longer exists.

The mission is continued by the newly formed Saint Matthew's United Methodist Church in nearby Madison. Now it has been expanded to include a back-to-school component. Boxes of gifts, clothes, bicycles, and food literally line the walls of the sanctuary and every hall of the building. Each gift and each box of food has someone's name on it. This past Christmas, gifts, toys, bicycles, and food found their way to just over 100 families that included almost 400 children.

Saint Matthew's mission statement reads: "We are a caring congregation reaching to people right where they are, relating them to Christ, and sending them out in the name of Christ."

The associate pastor, Sylvia Blackwell, says "Birthday Gifts for Christ" is Saint Matthew's signature ministry. "It is what we are all about, and it is what we want to be!" She shares this story:

"In November of 1997, a woman spoke at Saint Matthew's about her work at a local community center. At the end of her presentation, through tears, she told her story about why she works tirelessly, even without pay at times. She said, 'You see, at Christmas time several years ago my daughter and I were hungry, we had no heat in our home, and no sign of hope for things for Christmas. Then two members of your church knocked on my door and asked me what I might like or need for Christmas. Through that life-changing experience I found the strength and contacts to complete my GED, find a job, and now, well, here I am, reaching out to others.'"

Model 130:

Churches establish center to serve low-income people.

Initiated by the Hattiesburg District superintendent, Edward Street Fellowship Center began its ministry March 15, 1979 as a tutorial program for third- and fourth-graders in one of the low-income areas of Hattiesburg. Tutors and financial support came from local United Methodist churches in the Hattiesburg area.

The vision that gave birth to the tutorial program later gave birth to a Girls' Club and a Boys' Club for youngsters from twelve to eighteen years of age. These two clubs have been meeting now for over ten years. They provide programs, relational experiences, and recreational opportunities for teenagers who also live in the low-income area of Hattiesburg.

In 1991, a day care center was established at Edward Street. Its purpose was to provide quality care for mothers who were seeking to improve their education and those who had minimum wage paying jobs and could not afford the cost of a regular day care center.

The Reverend Clint Gill, president of the center's board of directors, says the center receives only about ten percent of its operating budget from fees paid by the mothers. Children are not turned down because of a mother's inability to pay. There's also a food pantry that gives emergency assistance.

Model 131:
Churches help low-income working mothers.

Lewisburg United Methodist Church, which has an average attendance of forty-five for Sunday worship, helps low-income working mothers by providing free child care for their school-age children during school holidays.

Called "God's Helpers for Working Mothers," the ministry began during the two week Christmas break in 1997.

Each day began with breakfast at seven o'clock and ended at three o'clock. Attendance ranged from seven to twenty children. Activities included arts and crafts, devotions, and play time. They took the children caroling, skating, to visit shut-in's at homes and in nursing homes. They also made trips to McDonald's for lunch.

It took four volunteers to manage the daily activities. The entire congregation pitched in to help with meals, snacks, and supplies. The children whose families could afford to contribute financially did so, and the families that could not afford to contribute did not.

"God's Helpers for Working Mothers" served again during spring break in 1998, and for the first time in many years, Lewisburg United Methodist Church was host for a vacation Bible school during the summer. A year ago, Lewisburg had only one child. Now it averages six children in church and has its first confirmation class in years. There are plans to hire a part-time staff to organize activities for the children and youth in the church and in the community.

Saint Luke's United Methodist Church in Tupelo held a similar program over spring break (1998). Saint Luke's offered supervised activities at no cost to eighteen children. All eighteen were from the larger community; none attended Saint Luke's.

Model 132:
Rural church serves unchurched children.

Pleasant Hill United Methodist Church is a rural congregation with an average worship attendance of seventy-five.

Four years ago, the church began to develop a vision for a children's ministry that might reach unchurched children. From that vision has grown a

Wednesday evening ministry that started with eleven children and now averages fifty.

Every Wednesday evening at five o'clock, the children gather for supervised recreation. At six o'clock they come together for fellowship and a meal. A retired music teacher provides a music program for the children, and at Christmas they put on their own Christmas play.

The church provides all of this at no cost to the children.

It takes a broad base of support from the congregation and about thirty committed volunteers. Pleasant Hill has purchased basketballs and basketball goals, volleyballs and a volleyball net, and other supplies. They remodeled their Sunday school rooms and even purchased a van.

Every Wednesday and Sunday the church van goes into the neighboring mobile home park and housing project to bring the children to church.

34.

Donelson Heights United Methodist Church
NASHVILLE, TENNESSEE

Model 133:

Nashville churches host homeless.

On a cold night more than a decade ago, a Catholic priest in Nashville invited some homeless people to sleep in his church. That's how Room in the Inn began. Now nearly 150 churches and organizations in Nashville participate in the ministry.

Rachel Hester, congregational coordinator for Room in the Inn, says that within recent years the denomination with the most congregations involved has been The United Methodist Church.

One of the participating United Methodist churches is Donelson Heights, a 500-member congregation where David Rainey is pastor. "We've been hosting Room in the Inn guests for five years," says David, "and by getting acquainted with people who have been with us, we've put some human faces to the homeless."

Every Wednesday from November through March, ten homeless people spend the night at Donelson Heights. They arrive at about five o'clock Wednesday afternoon, in time for an evening meal and a program that's usually attended by about 125 people from the church.

"We haven't sat down and designed something especially for our homeless guests," says David. "Instead, we invite them to join us for dinner and our evening activities. Some decline because they are exhausted from being on the street all day and are anxious to get some sleep, but quite a few join us. While we sit around the dinner table and talk with one another and share joys and concerns, our misconceptions about one another begin to clear up. We see one another in a new way."

David says the church nursery is helpful to homeless families. "Just to have somebody else hold the baby for a few minutes gives parents a break.

For the children, we have crafts, singing, Bible study, all kinds of programs are going on during the evening."

Being a host for Room in the Inn involves a number of adults: drivers to take guests to and from the Room in the Inn center, cooks to prepare the evening meal, breakfast and a sack lunch, plus a couple to spend the night at the church with the homeless.

Children and youth get involved too. "Sometimes our children make the sack lunches that we give our guests to take with them," David said. "For several years, our youth have had a chili cook-off, and they use the proceeds to buy Christmas gifts for our Room in the Inn guests."

Meeting children who are homeless has been an eye-opener for David's own children, who are three and thirteen "My kids go home to a warm house and they have more things than they know what to do with. Of course, homeless kids seldom know where they are going to sleep or what they are going to eat. My kids told me about meeting a little boy who guards his sister's shoes to make sure they aren't stolen in shelters or on the streets. Sometimes my kids have trouble keeping up with their shoes too, but for a different reason."

For middle-class United Methodists and homeless people to see one another in a new way, David is convinced, is one of the major benefits of Room in the Inn ministry. He feels strongly that involving the homeless people with the church people is vitally important.

35.

Stephan Memorial United Methodist Church
SAINT LOUIS, MISSOURI

Model 134:
St. Louis churches also host homeless.

The Room in the Inn model that was created in Nashville has spread to several other cities, where it has been modified to fit local needs and renamed.

In Saint Louis, Missouri, the ministry is called Room at the Inn, and it is a major resource of caring for homeless people in Saint Louis County.

One major difference: In Nashville the ministry is limited to the coldest months—November through March; in Saint Louis, it continues year round.

Another difference: The Saint Louis model offers more comprehensive services than Nashville offers at this time to help homeless people find long-term solutions to their problems. The Saint Louis model includes a component that works out of a Catholic church that gives the homeless job training and helps them find jobs and permanent housing.

When The Room at the Inn model began about five years ago, one of the first United Methodist churches to take part was Stephan Memorial. Located in a transitional neighborhood near the airport in Saint Louis County, the church has about 350 members. Their pastor is Mary Harvey, whose husband, Mark Harvey, ministers at Kingdom House, a United Methodist institution in Saint Louis that provides comprehensive ministries to the poor and marginalized.

Mary told me how The Room in the Inn model works at Stephan Memorial:

"At about 4:30 p.m. on the day our church is to be a host, we send a couple of cars over to the day shelter, and pick up ten people—usually that's two or three families. We have a host and a hostess who are at the church to greet them. We serve them dinner. After we eat, usually we have videos or

118

play cards or just visit. When our guests are ready to go to sleep, we have mattresses that we put on the floor for them and for the host and hostess. The next morning they have to get up fairly early. We serve them a simple breakfast, give them a sack lunch, and then the drivers take them back to the day shelter."

Mary acknowledges that going to a different church every night, instead of staying in one place for several nights, must be stressful to the homeless. "But," she says, "it's safer and healthier than sleeping on the street."

How does The Room in the Inn benefit the church? Mary told me:

"Most of our middle-class Methodist folks seldom really talk to poor people. But this ministry puts them in a setting where they eat with homeless people, talk with them through the evening, sleep in the church with them. And during the time they are together, they begin to realize that homeless people are people.

"Seeing what we see sometimes breaks our hearts. One night we had a woman with an eight-week old baby whose husband had deserted them. Another night we had a woman in her twenties who had been a college student. One evening while she was at a friend's home, she was shot in the leg during a drive-by shooting. She had all these medical complications and she didn't have insurance and because of all this she was out in the street."

Mary says when her members take part in this ministry, they not only become more aware of the plight of homeless people, they also become more aware of how fortunate they are, and problems that had been bothering them suddenly seem much more manageable.

36.

United Methodists Build for Homeless
NORTH GEORGIA ANNUAL CONFERENCE

Model 135:
Churches build houses for homeless.

During the 1997 session of the North Georgia Annual Conference, Bishop G. Lindsey Davis issued a challenge that some people thought would never be achieved.

The challenge: Receive a $120,000 offering while the conference was in session to fund a transitional home for a family in crisis in each of the twelve districts.

What happened? The special offering totaled $175,000, surpassing the original goal by more than $50,000.

At the 1998 annual conference session, it was announced that construction was underway on thirty housing units—two and one-half times the initial target goal of twelve.

"The offering gave us the base to really be serious about starting some housing for people, particularly families with children," says the Reverend Frank Windom, director of Urban Action, North Georgia Conference's umbrella agency that oversees outreach programs in metro Atlanta, August, Athens, Gainesville, and Rome.

The transitional housing program is a key part of the conference's response to the Children and Poverty Initiative launched in 1996 by the United Methodist Council of Bishops.

In addition to housing units, other programs are growing out of the Initiative. The Atlanta-Decatur-Oxford District, for example, is planning to provide literacy training for young mothers.

37.

Bluefield United Methodist Parish
BLUEFIELD, WEST VIRGINIA

Mary's Cradle Maternal and Infant Resource Center is the ministry of Bluefield (West Virginia) Parish, which consists of five churches whose memberships range from fifty to 400.

The ministry is directed by Marilyn Benson, a church and community worker employed by the United Methodist General Board of Global Ministries. Her assignment is to be involved in outreach ministries and to help the five churches of the parish minister to and with children and their families.

Marilyn says the primary mission of Mary's Cradle is to "respond to the needs of at-risk pregnant women, new mothers and their families by means of direct services and systemic change."

Mary's Cradle began during Advent in 1995. "We opened basically to provide maternity clothes and infant clothing and furniture and supplies for low-income people," Marilyn explained. "But we keep discovering other needs, and our ministry continues to grow."

Here are some examples of ministries Mary's Cradle provides. Each is a model that your church might consider.

Model 136:
Provide special-sized clothing.

"In the population we serve there is a higher incidence of low-birth weight babies, and so we try to provide special size clothing that these infants need," says Marilyn.

"We have a women's group in one of our churches that makes premature baby clothes. They use doll clothes patterns because they can't find any child clothes patterns that are small enough.

"When we give clothing to a mom, we suggest that she return it to us when her child outgrows it if the garment still has wear in it. Then we will give her child a bigger size, and put the one she returned back into our inventory. A lot of moms not only bring back clothes that they don't need any longer, they also bring us additional items that their friends or family have discarded.

Social workers from the Department of Human Services or other agencies often come in behalf of the mother and baby to get clothing and distribute it.

Model 137:
Ministry provides infant stimulation toys.

"Working with DHS, we learned that there was a special need for infant stimulation toys, everything from rattles and little squeaky toys on up to larger toys that are musical and move."

Marilyn explains that in West Virginia, no state or federal funds are available for these items, so if the family can't afford them the children may not have the toys. She says infant stimulation toys are especially needed by infants who have some kind of developmental delay. How does she find out who needs these items? Physicians and social workers contact her when they see people with such needs.

Model 138:
Ministry provides a lending library.

Books are gathered from various sources and made available for mother's and their children to provide enrichment and stimulation, as well as entertainment.

Model 139:
Ministry sponsors support group for moms.

Helping Young Moms Survive (HYMS) is a program that enables a pregnant or parenting teen to obtain needed items for herself and her baby while she is in school.

"If a mother's child becomes ill, and she takes him to the doctor, her medical card will cover that visit and any prescriptions the doctor gives her. But if the doctor says the child needs a vaporizer, the vaporizer is not covered. Our program helps provide those kinds of things."

Why is this support important. Marilyn explains: "Sometimes an expense for something like a vaporizer might be the straw that breaks the camel's back—all that it would take to cause a teen to drop out of school and take a low-paying job with no future."

Model 140:
Ministry sponsors overnight camp for moms and babies.

The purpose of this ministry, says Marilyn, is to give teen moms an opportunity to do some things that other teens do—such as go to camp and have fun while feeling secure about the care of their infant.

Included with the fun are enrichment activities, discussions about issues that are particularly important to teenage mothers. Another valuable benefit: The camp provides peer support for teens to get acquainted with others who have similar needs and concerns. They discover they are not alone. They know the church cares—and God cares.

How do five churches carry on such an extensive ministry? Marilyn says people are eager to be part of a project that they can see makes a positive difference in the lives of children and their moms.

"One of our churches that has only fifty members is really taking this ministry seriously," Marilyn says. "They find all kinds of ways to help. For example, they go to yard sales and buy baby cribs and baby clothes, and bring them here for us to pass along."

Many children and children's groups also help. "A Scout group had some community service money and went out and bought clothes and toys for babies. A junior high youth group washed used toys that had been given. Boys and girls in middle school—in the family and consumer science class, what we used to call home economics—made twelve baby quilts for us. This ministry lightens loads and brightens lives for a lot of teens, but people on the giving end received tremendous satisfaction from it too."

She says another key to developing Mary's Cradle has been the development of excellent relationship with agencies in the community that relate to early childhood. She works closely with the Department of Human Services, with public school teachers and counselors, and with various others who are concerned about children.

Marilyn believes that practically any church could adapt the models of ministry that Mary's Cradle provides. "You could do them at various levels, depending on your local needs and your church's resources."

38.

Rising Hope United Methodist Church
FAIRFAX COUNTY, VIRGINIA

It's a Sunday morning in the winter of 1997. About fifty people who are homeless or who have been homeless are gathered at Rising Hope—a storefront church in a shopping center. Worshiping with them is the bishop of the Virginia Conference, Joe Pennel Jr.

The pastor, Keary Kincannon, reminds his congregation that God is present in their lives whether they are aware of it or not, whether they are having a good day or a bad day. He asks, "Where has God been present in your life this past week? When have you felt the need for God the most?"

A woman in her thirties stands.

"I need to be taken to the detox center," she says. "I started using drugs again, and I had to prostitute myself to get the money to do the drugs, and I don't want to do either one again. I've come here for help."

She talks about her boyfriend. She is disturbed because he has not been treating her right, but she's also angry at herself because she feels she has not treated him right either.

She stops speaking and sits down. Immediately, Keary, Bishop Pennel and the congregation gather around her. They lay hands on her and pray for her. They pray God will heal her, that God will give her the strength to go through the detox program and to remain off drugs. They pray that she will soon find a good job, and that her relationship with her boyfriend will be healed. A few minutes later, the service ends and Keary takes her to the detox center.

That's an example of the kind of ministry that happens at Rising Hope. In Keary's words, "God is doing some wonderful things here! We are not only a church that ministers to the poor, we are also a church of the poor. Our congregation is made up almost entirely of low-income families and individuals who have found themselves in a shelter or on the streets."

Keary is convinced that Rising Hope is a ministry God has called into being. And he's grateful to be its pastor. In fact, it's the kind of church he has felt God calling him to serve. After graduating from Wesley Theological Seminary in Washington, D.C. in 1981, he worked nearly a decade with Sojourner's in Washington, ministering with the low-income community. Then he founded and directed for seven years a coalition that helped churches develop outreach ministries to the homeless.

"I was confused," Keary said. "I was feeling the call to continue serving the poor, but I was also feeling the call back to the pastorate." He shared his concern with Douglas Dillard Jr., superintendent of the Alexandria District, who in turn talked to the resident bishop of the Virginia Conference.

Soon the district superintendent came back to Keary, and explained that the Virginia Annual Conference didn't have any churches that were primarily ministering to the poor.

"When Dr. Dillard said that, I was ready to say okay, and go on about the work I had been doing," Keary said. "But then he smiled and told me, 'Let's start one. Let's start a church that's primarily for the poor.' It was wonderful to hear the church I had grown up in, The United Methodist Church, say, 'We recognize this call on your life and on the life of The United Methodist Church, and we want to make this happen.'"

Dillard placed a plan in motion to establish the church as a mission of the Alexandria District, which includes fifty-three churches located south of Washington. A ministry board was established to do whatever it took to establish the church and to give it oversight and support.

Jeff Henderson and his wife Nancy are co-chairs of that board. A retired couple, they bring a wealth of experience to the task. For years, Jeff was national chief of employment for the Internal Revenue Service, and later he was district manager for Public Storage Management. He's also a brigadier general in the Army Reserves. Nancy was chair for twenty-three years of the home economics department at a Fairfax County high school that has 4,000 students.

Jeff tells me that the ministry board had little trouble determining where the proposed church for the poor should be located. It was needed in Fairfax County to serve homeless and economically disadvantaged people along the Route One Corridor south of Washington.

"Fairfax County is one of the wealthiest counties in the nation," Jeff pointed out. "It borders Washington, it's where a lot of industries, especially defense contractors, have their headquarters. But there's a pocket of poverty along Route One. In fact, 23 percent of the people along Route One live at or below the poverty line."

He explained that Route One was the main artery into Washington until Interstate 95 was built about 1965. "When the Interstate opened, the motels and tourist courts that had prospered along Route One lost practically all their business and started falling into disrepair. Before long, the poor moved in and started living in the motels and tourist courts because the rates were so low. The area deteriorated for about twenty years, but right now it's being improved economically."

The support board for Route One Corridor ministry decided to locate the new church in the office complex of a shopping center near the people they hoped to serve. They rented a suite that provides space for a reception room, food distribution room, library, computer lab, children's room, office manager's office, director's office, and sanctuary.

Rising Hope was chartered June 9, 1996. With Keary as the founding pastor, the church has growing steadily. By August 1998, it had about fifty members and was providing on-going services to another 200 or so. Keary says most of the congregation and probably 90 percent of the people the church serves are still on the streets, doubled up with friends or neighbors, or living in a shelter, subsidized housing, or low-rent motels, apartments, and trailer parks.

Rising Hope's congregation—like all congregations—includes a variety of people. The church's membership is 48 percent white, 48 percent black, 2 percent Hispanic, and 2 percent Asian.

"Most of our people are working hard at minimum-wage jobs struggling to support themselves and their families" Keary says. "We have people here who are holding down full-time jobs, but they can't find any place to live that they can afford. Those without jobs are working hard at finding jobs."

Very few Rising Hope members have a church background, Keary says. "Out of our fifty members, only two transferred in from other United Methodist churches, and one was my wife. Only three came from other denominations. I have baptized more adults than children. None of the other members have ever really been active in a church before. And now they are our leaders."

One adult Keary baptized is Larry Payne, who is fifty-two. After Keary baptized him, he turned to the congregation and shared his story. "Before I quit drinking," he said, "I used to raise all kinds of hell. I landed in prison for some of my actions. But I thank God that He is my strength to stay off the booze and that He brought me to Rising Home."

Keary believes the people of Rising Hope need to do as much as they can for themselves. He says giving them opportunities for leadership helps them discover that they have leadership skills. As they serve others in the name of Christ, they are healed and grow.

"We are a ministry that really seeks to empower the poor. We work with them at the point where they need us to work with them," Keary points out. "If they need food or clothing, we try to provide it. If they need assistance getting a job, we help them identify their skills and strengths, and coach them on how to do good interviews. I'll be a reference when they need me.

We try to make sure they are checking the newspapers for job listings and putting in applications. Looking for a job can be disappointing. We encourage folks to keep trying. We've also been able to open some doors so people can get into housing programs and be assisted through various programs that are available."

The church has been declared a Community of Shalom by the General Board of Global Ministries of The United Methodist Church. Keary says their Shalom Zone's vision is to work collaboratively with other churches, community organizations, business, and government leaders to empower the grassroots, low-income leaders and residents to get involved in planning for their community's future.

When we examine how Rising Hope ministers to and with the poor, we can discover several models for ministry that can be effective elsewhere, perhaps in your local church.

Does Rising Hope have a big staff? No. In addition to the pastor, there's only one other person who receives pay—the office manager. How does a two-person staff carry on such a demanding ministry?

"We have scores of volunteers, at least three or four on any given day," Keary says. "They help our people make sure they are going through the right process to get the public and private services that are available for them. They help our people learn to do budgets and teach them how to maintain an apartment. Many volunteers are mentors."

Even though it is charted as a United Methodist church, Rising Hope is a mission of the Alexandria District. "The churches of our district see us as a mission in their own backyard," Keary says. "They support us both financially and with volunteers."

Model 141:
Needy get food and prayer.

Rising Hope provides bags of groceries each week to more than 100 families—at least 250 people. "When we give the groceries," Keary says, "we ask the person receiving them if he or she has any prayer concerns. They nearly always do. We find a quiet place and pray with them. Lots of times the prayer seems to mean more to them than the groceries."

The last Wednesday of every month, Rising Hope hosts a free pancake and sausage supper for anyone who walks in from the street. United Methodist churches in the Alexandria District take turns providing the meals.

"After the meal, we have a praise service of spirited music and witness to the activity of Jesus Christ in our lives," Keary says. "We advertise by passing our flyers at the shopping centers, bus stops, shelters, and motels along Route One. Our attendance is usually about sixty, and we have gained several new members as a result."

Model 142:
Voluteers staff transportation ministry.

Since few of the people served by Rising Hope have cars, the church has a transportation ministry. Frequently, volunteers from other United Methodist churches of Alexandria District drive people to medical, legal, social work, or job appointments. Sometimes they take the elderly and handicapped to grocery stores. Occasionally, volunteers with pick-up trucks haul trash to the dump or pick up furniture that has been donated to Rising Hope or its members.

Model 143:
Clothing ministry addresses need.

Rising Hope's clothing closet ministry serves more than 100 families a month. When they have a Saturday sidewalk clothing give-a-way, they usually serve more than 200. Clothes are donated by members of United Methodist churches in the district, and members of the churches also help maintain and coordinate this ministry.

Model 144:
Church partners with other United Methodist churches.

Rising Hope partners with other United Methodist churches, and together they reach far more people than they could ever reach alone.

With the support of Aldersgate UMC, Rising Hope in 1997 held a Christmas party for seventy-five children from the public housing projects, the shelters, and trailer parks that dot the Route One corridor.

Aldersgate provided the space, the crafts and the transportation. Sydenstricker UMC provided a clown. Saint Matthew's UMC provided hundreds of candy poppers. Manassas/Saint Thomas UMC made sure that every child had a Christmas gift. Christ UMC provided punch and cookies. Rising Hope provide the Santa and the music.

Several needy children and adults received at least one present last Christmas because of the many Christmas Angels that donated a gift through Rising Hope. Christ UMC put up an Angel Tree with the names and needs of fifty people served by Rising Hope. Aldersgate UMC took ten children from Route One shopping for their families. Immanuel UMC provided 100 softballs. Woodlawn UMC made several children's gifts. Christmas meals were made available by several churches. Many of the homeless on the streets and in the shelters were blessed with one of the shoe boxes of toiletries, candies, scarves, hats, and gloves provided by Saint Paul UMC. Dumfries UMC warmed many homeless children and adults by providing 150 coats. Aldersgate UMC provided twelve Christmas trees to families with young children.

Model 145:
Partner church sponsors day camp.

Every summer, Burke United Methodist Church hosts a two-week day camp for children from the Rising Hope community who are between four and ten. Burke is located in a wooded area with a lake. The campers do everything from read Bible stories to engage in crafts and go fishing.

"Our parents say going to the day camp has been one of the most exciting things their kids have done," says Keary. "Some great relationships are established. Junior and senior high youth from Burke are paired up with Rising Hope children. So our children really have mentors and special friends they can be with during that whole week, and at the end, its tough for them to leave. You see kids from both churches hugging and crying because they have been so touched by the experience."

Model 146:
Vacation Bible school carried to housing project.

Volunteers from Alexandria District churches also assist with Rising Hope's vacation Bible school. Obviously, there's not room in Rising Hope's shopping center location for a VBS. So they hold it at a much better location: in the middle of a nearby public housing project, where its more convenient for the children it is designed to serve.

"We met in the family resource center at the project," says Keary. "Last summer we had sixty children from the project. About thirty youth and adults from Aldersgate volunteered to help us. It was a great experience for all of us."

Model 147:
Sunday school meets Tuesday evening.

Since few members of Rising Hope have a church background, they are not yet comfortable teaching church school classes. To help meet this need, volunteers from other United Methodist churches teach classes. And since the volunteers are involved on Sundays in their own churches, Rising Hope has its church school on Tuesday evenings.

Model 148:
Christian care groups provide ongoing assistance.

Keary says many people come to him for counseling, but a few one-on-one sessions are not enough to address some of their needs. That's why Rising Hope has established Christian care groups that work with people week after week on issues with which they are struggling. A pastor in a neighboring church and a Christian counselor assist with the Christian care group.

Model 149:
Church's hospitality encourages members' hospitality.

Apparently, when Rising Hope members see churches working together to extend hospitality, it motivates them to share with others. Last Christmas, one Rising Hope member invited six people who would otherwise have spent Christmas alone into her home for dinner. Another member who lives in public housing recognized that many are depressed and alone on Thanksgiving. With the support of Rising Hope, she invited thirty people—many were homeless—to her home for turkey and football.

Model 150:
Music ministry develops discipline.

On Keary's drawing board as this book goes to press is a plan to develop an after-school music program for children and youth. Why? One reason is to draw to the church children and youth who love music and want to learn to play, but don't have an instrument or a teacher. Studies show that learning a musical instrument helps children develop discipline, and the more discipline they develop, the more their grades—and their lives—improve.

Keary is now going to different churches in the area, inviting people who know how to play musical instruments to volunteer to teach in the after school-program. He's also encouraging people who have musical instruments stuck back in their closets to bring them over to the church, promising that they will be put to good use.

"We'll invite the children and youth who want to learn to play an instrument to come over a couple afternoons each week when they get out of school and study with our volunteer music teachers," Keary explains. "We'll make sure we do the kind of music the kids like to do, not just the rote stuff or the classical. As we develop musicians, we will bring them into the church service. I'm up there with my guitar most Sundays, trying to get things going. Having some kids play keyboards and base guitars and drums and other instruments would be tremendous for the kids and for our church."

Several other social service agencies work with low income people up and down the Route One corridor in Fairfax County. What makes Rising Hope unique? Here's Keary's explanation:

"We are not a social service agency. We are a church. So our basic empowerment in the community starts at a spiritual level. We meet people's needs with food and clothing and that sort of thing, but we don't stop there. We want to be a place that offers hope, a place that counters the despair that so many in the community face. So we work at a spiritual level.

"We have to start with the spiritual, that's the core. When people get surrounded by the darkness, when they get totally disillusioned and despairing, when there's no direction in their lives and no hope, they are literally lost. We have to help them open the door up to Christ so they can realize that there is hope, that Christ does offer a way to a better life. When we work with them at the spiritual level, they begin to recognize that God does care about them. And once they recognize that God cares, they are on solid ground. They have a reason for hope. Their self-esteem and self-confidence grows."

Rising Hope's pastor and leaders realize that to help others grow spiritually they must also grow spiritually. To stimulate their own spiritual growth, Keary and several church officers have formed a leadership care group.

"We use John Wesley's historical questions that were asked of the class meetings and some other covenant questions that we have come up with for ourselves," Keary explains.

"So at each of our meetings, we ask ourselves questions like these: Since we met last, how have I sinned? What temptations have I met? How is God working in my life to overcome these temptations? And then we move on to some other questions that get at personal spiritual growth, helping us recognize that we don't have to remain in our sin, but that we can begin to be empowered by God to improve our lives through God's power.

"We ask ourselves: Since we last met, what acts of mercy have I done? What acts of justice have I done? What acts of devotion have I done? What acts of worship? So we try to recognize that as the healing is taking place in our lives, we are also to begin moving into world and trying to help others experience God's healing."

United Methodists in the Alexandria District of Virginia Conference—most of whom are middle-to upper-income people—could close their eyes to the needs of the poor who live along Route One. But they are responding to this pocket of poverty, thanks to clergy and lay people of vision and compassion.

Even though their churches are not located in low-income areas, they still minister to children and their families who are struggling financially by partnering with churches that are in pockets of poverty. As Keary points out, a church does not have to be in a low-income neighborhood to minister to low-income people. Through our United Methodist connectional system, we are structured for partnership ministries that enable us to reach all kinds of people in all kinds of places.

Part Five

Characteristics of a Child-Friendly Church

39.

Love and Respect Children

The churches featured in previous chapters vary in size, in settings, and in other significant ways. But when we reflect upon them, I think we can identify three characteristics that all child-friendly churches have in common. The first: they love and respect kids.

Don't all churches everywhere love and respect kids?

Unfortunately, some don't. At least many kids think they don't, according to Shirley Paschal, program director for the PeaceMaking Academy at Grace United in Kansas City, profiled in chapter 25.

"I'm not trying to put our churches in a bad light because lots of churches are doing great things for kids, including kids in gangs," Shirley told me candidly. "I'm proud of those churches. But we have some churches where folks in charge don't want anybody around—especially kids—unless they dress and act just right. We've come up with all kinds of ways to put people down and make them feel that they don't belong. We have pushed them out of our way, pretended they are not there."

Shirley understands how inner-city children with whom she works think and feel. Poverty, prejudice, abuse, violence, drug addiction, and alcoholism are not just topics she has read about in textbooks. She has experienced them personally and she has observed their impact on children and youth.

"After working with this population for a long time, I can tell you that young people in gangs are just young people with problems and issues and concerns that they don't see an answer to. Many of them have been alienated or excluded by the rest of society. So they have banned together. They believe they have to be there for each other because no one else is there for them. They feel left out, and frankly for the most part they are left out."

Shirley says young people in gangs are not the only people who are frequently stereotyped by churches. "We put down African Americans, Asian Americans, Latinos, and other people of color. We also put down children and people of all ages who are poor, who are old, who are in wheelchairs, who are in prisons, who are homosexuals, who have AIDS, and the list goes on. I'm sure that many times we put kids down without intending to put them down and without even realizing that we are putting them down, but the kids still feel put down."

I asked her how churches can win the respect and trust of children and youth who are convinced that the church is not child-friendly.

"We can't do it by putting on that we care when we don't," she replied without hesitation. "We've got to really care for kids. We've got to follow the example of Jesus. How did Jesus treat the lepers and the other people who were put down? He lifted them up. And that's what we need to do with children and people of all ages who have been put down by our society. We must lift them up! How do we lift them up? We let them see by our attitudes and by our actions that we respect them as God's children and as our brothers and sisters. We show them we trust them by giving them responsibilities, by risking ourselves a little. When they see that we really believe in them, before long they start believing in themselves. They open their minds to seeing and thinking in a different way. They discover their strengths. They begin to realize that they are persons of worth—that they are God's children. And that God loves them just the way they are and will help them become the best they can be."

40.

Respond to Children's Needs

Here's the second characteristic of child-friendly churches: They respond to the needs of children in the church and in the community.

Rather than guessing what children need, the child friendly churches we have examined do research to determine what children need. And they don't limit their research to church kids; they are concerned about the needs of unchurched kids too. Then they determine what resources their church has that God can use to address those needs, and they minister with those resources. An excellent model: East Tenth in Indianapolis, featured in chapter 24.

Virginia Annual Conference of The United Methodist Church uses regional children's issue forums to identify needs and inform people of what is happening to children in their local communities as well as statewide and nationally.

"We pull together churches from several neighboring districts," says Kathie Allport, a member of the Virginia Conference children's issue committee that coordinates the forums.

Most of the people who attend are Sunday school teachers and church school directors, church and society people, pastors, and directors of Christian education. Many are parents. "All the people who come have at least one thing in common," says Allport: "They want the best for our children."

Typically, a forum features presentations from six to eight residents of the local communities who have worked with children and youth for years. Most are juvenile justice, education, health, welfare, substance abuse, and counseling professionals.

"We ask each presenter to speak ten minutes or less on what he or she believes is the one most critical issue affecting children and youth in our area," explains Allport. "We have a timekeeper and we are pretty rigid about sticking to our schedule. We also ask each speaker to give us in advance an abstract of his or her remarks and we put these in a collection."

Virginia Conference's first children's issue forum was held in Richmond in 1995. Since then, they have had two a year. To plan the regional forums, a local committee is formed and works closely with the conference children's issue committee. The local committee recruits speakers from the community and helps with promotion and other local arrangements.

41.

Leave the Miracles to God

Here's the third characteristic that the child-friendly churches featured in previous chapters have in common: After ministering faithfully to and with children, they leave the miracles to God.

Hobson Church in Nashville, featured in chapter 19, is an excellent example. To determine what it means to minister faithfully, they began by studying the Bible, searching for insights that would help them become more aware of and more committed to the mission of Christ's church. Then they used the biblical images of the church as guidelines to design, implement and evaluate their ministries. The rest they left with God.

While doing research for this book, I have been inspired by many leaders of child-friendly churches who are ministering faithfully in difficult settings and trusting God to bring forth good from their efforts. Perhaps the one who has inspired me most is the Reverend Sharon Garfield, pastor of Grace United Church in Kansas City, Missouri.

Sharon wears many hats. One—by no means her favorite—is the fund raiser hat. Obviously, a hunk of her church's budget goes for maintenance and utilities. The church building, which is nearly 100 years old, has fifty-seven rooms and a big sanctuary. Operating more than a dozen community ministries that serve about 2,500 people each month takes money—much more than can be provided by the 250 members of the congregation, some of whom are unemployed and most of whom skimp by on incomes below the poverty level.

Where does the money for her church come from? Some is from foundations and humanitarian agencies concerned about people in the inner city, but most comes from the United Methodist and Presbyterian churches. Since Grace Church is affiliated with these two denominations, it receives some missional support from both, but keeping their support depends on keeping them aware of the church's ministry and needs.

One chilly November afternoon about three o'clock, Sharon was preparing for a visit from a denominational executive who was coming to discuss the church's request for much needed financial assistance. She heard someone knock on the front door. She thought it might be the denominational executive, but when she opened the door she saw a man in his mid-twenties she had never seen before. He was scruffy and smelly and was obviously intoxicated.

"He told me he wanted food," Sharon recalls. "I explained to him that our food pantry was closed and suggested that he come back the next morning. He got very belligerent and started yelling that he was hungry now and that it was my responsibility to feed him now."

Sharon says that as the man vented his rage on her, she lost control. "Quite truthfully, it made me pretty angry that he would give me an ultimatum. I just wasn't in the mood to hear it. Why didn't he come during our hours? I had an important meeting to prepare for. I didn't have time for this!

"I wanted to get rid of him, so I could get ready for my meeting. So I told him, 'Okay, I'll get you some food.' Then I did something that I'm not proud of. I had never done it before and I've never done it since. Instead of letting him come in the church, I slammed the door in his face and ran down to the food pantry and got some stuff off the shelves, just as little as possible.

"When I got to the door to give him the food, I discovered something was blocking the door. I got it open a little and much to my horror, I could see that the man from the Presbytery had just pulled up in front of the church and was getting out of his car. Then I saw why the door wouldn't open. The young man had fallen over and was laying in front of it. I kept pushing on the door, trying to get it open, and eventually did. I knelt down beside the young man, and tried to wake him up and get him up, hoping I could at least move him before the executive got there.

"That's when something happened that I can not explain. Something unlike anything I had ever experienced. I was kneeling down close to this young man, pushing him and shaking him, and suddenly it was as though I saw in his face the face of Jesus. And I heard him mumble, 'All I wanted was to be heard.' Immediately I thought of what Jesus said, 'When you do it unto the least of these my brothers and sisters you have done it until me.' That shocked me into remembering what I was called for and what the church is really to be about."

Sharon looked up and saw the denominational executive standing beside her. Suddenly, her appointment with him didn't seem all that important. She briefly greeted him, invited him to go inside and visit with people from the church. And then she turned her attention to what seemed to be all that mattered at that moment: ministering to this young man.

Within a few minutes, Sharon and the young man were inside the church, drinking hot coffee. He was eating a sandwich and becoming more aware of where he was and what was going on.

As Sharon sat with him, he told her his story. He said his mother had recently died of cancer. While she was sick, he had quit his job to take care of her because there was no one else in the family who could, and hiring someone to stay with her would have cost much more than he could make at his minimum wage job. He said he believed his mother could have lived if she had gotten the medical care she needed, but she didn't have the money and didn't have insurance and couldn't qualify for any more public assistance. He had seen her be a very giving person, very caring all her life. Yet when she was in trouble no one was there for her. He talked about how angry he got watching his mother literally die. He was convinced that nobody cared if his mother lived or died. And that God—if there really was a God—evidently didn't care either. He said he had been trying to find a job, but nobody would hire him. He said he felt alone and hopeless. He said that when his mom died, it was like something snapped and he started drinking and never stopped.

Sharon had heard stories like his many times. She didn't lecture him for thinking like a victim and blaming all his problems on others. She didn't scold him for questioning God's existence. She didn't offer any pat answers to his problems. Instead, she simply listened emphatically as he vented his anger and frustration and fear.

As she listened, she hoped that he would sense how much she cared and how much God cared, and become aware that he was never alone, that God was always with him. After he had finished expressing his deepest feelings, she told him she would like to help him find a job and invited him to come back the next morning.

"I didn't know if he would come back or not," says Sharon. "But sure enough the next morning he came. He had shaved and was wearing clean clothes and was sober. We talked about his future. I told him about a job opening, and asked him if he would like for me to set up an interview. He said yes, and left the church, appearing to be excited and hopeful."

I asked Sharon how the young man is doing now.

"I wish I could tell you that he got the job, that he hasn't taken a drink, that he's now an active member of our church, and that he is going to live happily ever after," Sharon replied. "But the truth is, I haven't seen or heard from him since he left for the interview. I don't know what's happened and I may never know."

Working for several decades with people like this young man has taught Sharon that she is powerless when it comes to fixing somebody's broken life. She knows that regardless of how much she wants to and despite how skillfully she tries, she can not control how another human being feels and thinks and acts.

How does she cope with this realization?

"I keep reminding myself that I'm not responsible for miracles," Sharon said. "Miracles are God's department. All I'm responsible for is my own life and living it as a faithful disciple."

"What do you think it means to be a faithful disciple?" I asked.

"Doing what Jesus did and what he commanded us to do," she replied. "We are called to be like the Good Samaritan Jesus told about and to care enough for others—including strangers and people who have gotten themselves in trouble—that we will make sacrifices and take risks to help them just as we would make sacrifices and take risks to help Jesus."

Sharon says she is confident of this: Even though we may never see all the seeds that we plant take root and grow, most of them will produce abundantly some day, some where, and some way. She has no doubt that God works in and through us, using our encouraging words, our kind acts, and our supportive spirits to heal people and to help them experience inner peace and joy.

"I've seen plenty of miracles happen around this church," Sharon concluded. "This is not a God-forsaken neighborhood. God lives here and God works here just as God lives and works everywhere else in the world."

Sharon is an example of one through whom God gives us a child-friendly church.